CAMBRIDGE LIBRARY

Books of enduring schol

Travel and Exploration

The history of travel writing dates back to the Bible, Caesar, the Vikings and the Crusaders, and its many themes include war, trade, science and recreation. Explorers from Columbus to Cook charted lands not previously visited by Western travellers, and were followed by merchants, missionaries, and colonists, who wrote accounts of their experiences. The development of steam power in the nineteenth century provided opportunities for increasing numbers of 'ordinary' people to travel further, more economically, and more safely, and resulted in great enthusiasm for travel writing among the reading public. Works included in this series range from first-hand descriptions of previously unrecorded places, to literary accounts of the strange habits of foreigners, to examples of the burgeoning numbers of guidebooks produced to satisfy the needs of a new kind of traveller - the tourist.

The Narrative of the Honourable John Byron, Commodore in a Late Expedition Round the World

John Byron (1723–86) died a vice-admiral, having earned the nickname 'Foulweather Jack' after much experience on rough seas. In 1741 he was a midshipman aboard H.M.S. *Wager* in a squadron sent to attack Spanish ships off Chile. Shipwrecked in a storm after rounding Cape Horn, the majority of the survivors turned on their captain and attempted to make their own way home. Byron was among the group who stayed with the commanding officer. In 1768, now a commodore, he published this account of the five harrowing years it took to get back to England, by which time he was one of only four survivors. Although no doubt written to give his side of the story, it appealed to a public eager for tales of dramatic endurance against the odds. Aboard the *Beagle* on Darwin's voyage, the book also informed the shipwreck in *Don Juan* by the author's grandson.

Cambridge University Press has long been a pioneer in the reissuing of out-of-print titles from its own backlist, producing digital reprints of books that are still sought after by scholars and students but could not be reprinted economically using traditional technology. The Cambridge Library Collection extends this activity to a wider range of books which are still of importance to researchers and professionals, either for the source material they contain, or as landmarks in the history of their academic discipline.

Drawing from the world-renowned collections in the Cambridge University Library and other partner libraries, and guided by the advice of experts in each subject area, Cambridge University Press is using state-of-the-art scanning machines in its own Printing House to capture the content of each book selected for inclusion. The files are processed to give a consistently clear, crisp image, and the books finished to the high quality standard for which the Press is recognised around the world. The latest print-on-demand technology ensures that the books will remain available indefinitely, and that orders for single or multiple copies can quickly be supplied.

The Cambridge Library Collection brings back to life books of enduring scholarly value (including out-of-copyright works originally issued by other publishers) across a wide range of disciplines in the humanities and social sciences and in science and technology.

The Narrative
of the Honourable
John Byron
Commodore in a Late
Expedition Round the World

Containing an Account of the Great Distresses
Suffered by Himself and his Companions
on the Coast of Patagonia, from the Year 1740,
till their Arrival in England, 1746

JOHN BYRON

CAMBRIDGE
UNIVERSITY PRESS

CAMBRIDGE
UNIVERSITY PRESS

University Printing House, Cambridge, CB2 8BS, United Kingdom

Published in the United States of America by Cambridge University Press, New York

Cambridge University Press is part of the University of Cambridge.
It furthers the University's mission by disseminating knowledge in the pursuit of
education, learning and research at the highest international levels of excellence.

www.cambridge.org
Information on this title: www.cambridge.org/9781108065368

© in this compilation Cambridge University Press 2013

This edition first published 1768
This digitally printed version 2013

ISBN 978-1-108-06536-8 Paperback

This book reproduces the text of the original edition. The content and language reflect
the beliefs, practices and terminology of their time, and have not been updated.

Cambridge University Press wishes to make clear that the book, unless originally published
by Cambridge, is not being republished by, in association or collaboration with, or
with the endorsement or approval of, the original publisher or its successors in title.

Titles known to have formed part of Charles Darwin's library during the *Beagle* voyage, available in the CAMBRIDGE LIBRARY COLLECTION

Abel, Clarke: *Narrative of a Journey in the Interior of China, and of a Voyage to and from that Country in the Years 1816 and 1817* (1818) [ISBN 9781108045995]

Aubuisson de Voisins, J.F. d': *Traité de Géognosie* (2 vols., 1819) [ISBN 9781108029728]

Bougainville, L. de, translated by John Reinhold Forster: *A Voyage Round the World, Performed by Order of His Most Christian Majesty, in the Years 1766–1769* (1772) [9781108031875]

Buch, Leopold von, translated by John Black, with notes and illustrations by Robert Jameson: *Travels through Norway and Lapland during the years 1806, 1807, and 1808* (1813) [ISBN 9781108028813]

Byron, John: *The Narrative of the Honourable John Byron, Commodore in a Late Expedition Round the World* (1768) [ISBN 9781108065368]

Caldcleugh, Alexander: *Travels in South America, during the Years, 1819–20–21* (2 vols., 1825) [ISBN 9781108033732]

Callcott, Maria (née Graham): *Voyage of H.M.S. Blonde to the Sandwich Islands, in the Years 1824–1825* (1826) [ISBN 9781108062114]

Candolle, Augustin Pyramus de, and Sprengel, Kurt: *Elements of the Philosophy of Plants* (1821) [ISBN 9781108037464]

Colnett, James: *A Voyage to the South Atlantic and Round Cape Horn into the Pacific Ocean* (1798) [ISBN 9781108048354]

Cuvier, Georges: *Le règne animal distribué d'après son organisation* (4 vols., 1817) [ISBN 9781108058872]

Cuvier, Georges, edited by Edward Griffith: *The Animal Kingdom* (16 vols., 1827–35) [ISBN 9781108049702]

Daniell, J. Frederic: *Meteorological Essays and Observations* (1827) [ISBN 9781108056571]

De la Beche, Henry T.: *A Selection of the Geological Memoirs Contained in the Annales des Mines* (1824) [ISBN 9781108048408]

Earle, Augustus: *A Narrative of a Nine Months' Residence in New Zealand in 1827* (1832) [ISBN 9781108039789]

Ellis, William: *Polynesian Researches during a Residence of Nearly Six Years in the South Sea Islands* (2 vols., 1829) [ISBN 9781108065382]

Falkner, Thomas: *A Description of Patagonia, and the Adjoining Parts of South America* (1774) [ISBN 9781108060547]

Fleming, John: *The Philosophy of Zoology* (2 vols., 1822) [ISBN 9781108001649]

Flinders, Matthew: *A Voyage to Terra Australis* (2 vols., 1814) [ISBN 9781108018203]

Forster, John Reinhold: *Observations Made During a Voyage Round the World* (1778) [ISBN 9781108031882]

Greenough, George Bellas: *Critical Examination of the First Principles of Geology* (1819) [ISBN 9781108035323]

Hawkesworth, John: *An Account of the Voyages Undertaken by the Order of His Present Majesty for Making Discoveries in the Southern Hemisphere* (3 vols., 1773) [ISBN 9781108065528]

Head, Francis Bond: *Rough Notes Taken during some Rapid Journeys across the Pampas and among the Andes* (1826) [ISBN 9781108001618]

Humboldt, Alexander von: *Essai géognostique sur le gisement des roches dans les deux hémisphères* (1826) [ISBN 9781108049481]

Humboldt, Alexander von, translated by J.B.B. Eyriès: *Tableaux de la nature* (1828) [ISBN 9781108052757]

Humboldt, Alexander von, translated by Helen Maria Williams: *Personal Narrative of Travels* (7 vols., 1814–29) [ISBN 9781108028004]

Humboldt, Alexander von: *Fragmens de géologie et de climatologie Asiatiques* (2 vols., 1831) [ISBN 9781108049443]

Jones, Thomas: *A Companion to the Mountain Barometer* (1817) [ISBN 9781108049375]

King, Phillip Parker: *Narrative of a Survey of the Intertropical and Western Coasts of Australia, Performed between the Years 1818 and 1822* (2 vols., 1827) [ISBN 9781108045988]

Kirby, William and Spence, William: *An Introduction to Entomology* (4 vols., 1815–26) [ISBN 9781108065597]

Kotzebue, Otto von, translated by H.E. Lloyd: *A Voyage of Discovery, into the South Sea and Beering's Straits, for the Purpose of Exploring a North-East Passage* (3 vols., 1821) [ISBN 9781108057608]

La Pérouse, Jean-François de Galaup de, edited by L.A. Millet-Mureau: *A Voyage Round the World, Performed in the Years 1785, 1786, 1787, and 1788, by the Boussole and Astrolabe* (2 vols., 1799) [ISBN 9781108031851]

Lamarck, Jean-Baptiste Pierre Antoine de Monet de: *Histoire naturelle des animaux sans vertèbres* (7 vols., 1815–22) [ISBN 9781108059084]

Lyell, Charles: *Principles of Geology* (3 vols., 1830–3) [ISBN 9781108001342]

Macdouall, John: *Narrative of a Voyage to Patagonia and Terra del Fuego* (1833) [ISBN 9781108060981]

Mawe, John: *Travels in the Interior of Brazil* (1821) [ISBN 9781108052788]

Miers, John: *Travels in Chile and La Plata* (2 vols., 1826) [ISBN 9781108072977]

Molina, Giovanni Ignazio: *The Geographical, Natural, and Civil History of Chili* (2 vols., 1782–6, English translation 1809) [ISBN 9781108049474]

Owen, William Fitzwilliam, translated by Heaton Bowstead Robinson: *Narrative of Voyages to Explore the Shores of Africa, Arabia, and Madagascar* (2 vols., 1833) [ISBN 9781108050654]

Pernety, Antoine-Joseph: *The History of a Voyage to the Malouine (or Falkland) Islands* (1770, English translation 1771) [ISBN 9781108064330]

Phillips, William: *An Elementary Introduction to the Knowledge of Mineralogy* (1816) [ISBN 9781108049382]

Playfair, John: *Illustrations of the Huttonian Theory of the Earth* (1802) [ISBN 9781108072311]

Scrope, George Poulett: *Considerations on Volcanos* (1825) [ISBN 9781108072304]

Southey, Robert: *History of Brazil* (3 vols., 1810–19) [ISBN 9781108052870]

Spix, Johann Baptist von, and Martius, C.F.P. von, translated by H.E. Lloyd: *Travels in Brazil, in the Years 1817–1820* (2 vols., 1824) [ISBN 9781108063807]

Turnbull, John: *A Voyage Round the World, in the Years 1800, 1801, 1802, 1803, and 1804* (1805, this edition 1813) [ISBN 9781108053983]

Ulloa, Antonio de, translated and edited by John Adams: *A Voyage to South America* (2 vols., 1806) [ISBN 9781108031707]

Volney, Constantin-François: *Voyage en Syrie et en Égypte pendant les années 1783, 1784 et 1785* (2 vols., 1787) [ISBN 9781108066556]

Webster, William Henry Bayley: *Narrative of a Voyage to the Southern Atlantic Ocean, in the Years 1828, 29, 30, Performed in H.M. Sloop Chanticleer* (2 vols., 1834) [ISBN 9781108041898]

Weddell, James: *A Voyage towards the South Pole: Performed in the Years 1822–24* (1825) [ISBN 9781108041584]

Wood, James: *The Elements of Algebra* (1815) [ISBN 9781108066532]

For a complete list of titles in the Cambridge Library Collection please visit: http://www.cambridge.org/features/CambridgeLibraryCollection/books.htm

THE HONOURABLE COMMODORE

JOHN BYRON's NARRATIVE.

THE
NARRATIVE

OF THE HONOURABLE

JOHN BYRON

(Commodore in a Late EXPEDITION round the WORLD)

CONTAINING

AN ACCOUNT

OF THE

GREAT DISTRESSES

Suffered by Himfelf and His Companions on the

COAST OF PATAGONIA,

From the Year 1740, till their Arrival in ENGLAND, 1746.

WITH A

DESCRIPTION of St. JAGO DE CHILI,

and the MANNERS and CUSTOMS of the INHABITANTS.

ALSO A

Relation of the Lofs of the WAGER Man of War,

One of ADMIRAL ANSON's Squadron.

WRITTEN BY HIMSELF,
And now Firft Publifhed.

LONDON:

Printed for S. BAKER and G. LEIGH, in York-ftreet; and
T. DAVIES, in Ruffel-ftreet, Covent-garden.
MDCCLXVIII.

PREFACE.

AS the greateſt pain I feel in committing the following ſheets to
the preſs, ariſes from an apprehenſion
that many of my readers will accuſe me
of egotiſm ; I will not incur that charge
in my preface, by detaining them with
the reaſons which have induced me, at
this time, to yield to the deſire of my
friends. It is equally indifferent to the
public to be told how it happened, that
nothing ſhould have got the better of
my indolence and reluctance to comply
with the ſame requeſts, for the ſpace of
twenty years.

I will employ theſe few introductory
pages merely to ſhew what pretenſions

A z 3.   this

this work may have to the notice of the world, after thofe publications which have preceded it.

It is well known that the Wager, one of lord Anfon's fquadron, was caft away upon a defolate ifland in the South-feas. The fubject of this book is a relation of the extraordinary difficulties and hard-fhips through which, by the affiftance of Divine Providence, a fmall part of her crew efcaped to their native land ; and a very fmall proportion of thofe made their way in a new and unheard of manner, over a large and defert tract of land between the weftern mouth of the Magellanic ftreight and the capital of Chili; a country fcarce to be paral-leled in any part of the globe, in that it affords neither fruits, grain, nor even roots proper for the fuftenance of man ; and what is ftill more rare, the very fea, which yields a plentiful fupport to many

a barren

a barren coaſt, on this tempeſtuous and inhoſpitable ſhore is found to be almoſt as barren as the land ; and it muſt be confeſſed, that to thoſe who cannot intereſt themſelves with ſeeing human nature labouring, from day to day, to preſerve its exiſtence under the continual want of ſuch real neceſſaries as food and ſhelter from the moſt rigorous climate, the following ſheets will afford but little entertainment.

Yet, after all, it muſt be allowed there can be no other way of aſcertaining the geography and natural hiſtory of a country which is altogether moraſs and rock, incapable of products or culture, than by ſetting down every minute circumſtance which was obſerved in traverſing it.   The ſame may be ſaid of the inhabitants, their manners, religion, and language.   What fruits could an European reap from a more intimate acquaintance

with

with them, than what he will find in the following accidental obfervations ? We faw the moft unprofitable fpot on the globe of the earth, and fuch it is defcribed and afcertained to be.

It is to be hoped fome little amends may be made by fuch an infight as is given into the interior part of the country ; and I find what I have put down has had the good fortune to be pleafing to fome of my friends ; infomuch that the only fault I have yet had laid to my papers is, that of being too fhort in the article of the Spanifh fettlements. But here I muft fay, I have been dubious of the partiality of my friends ; and, as I think, juftly fearful left the world in general, who may perhaps find compaf-fion and indulgence for a protracted tale of diftrefs, may not give the fame allow-ance to a luxurious imagination tri-umphing in a change of fortune, and

fudden

sudden tranfition from the moft difmal
to the gayeft fcenes in the univerfe, and
thereby indulging an egotifm equally
offenfive to the envious and cenforious.

I fpeak as briefly as poffible of matters previous to our final feparation from
the reft of lord Anfon's fquadron; for
it is from this epocha that the train of
our misfortunes properly commences:
and though Mr. Bulkeley, one of the
warrant officers of the Wager, has long
fince publifhed a Journal and Account
of the return of that part of the fhip's
company, which, diffenting from captain Cheap's propofal of endeavouring
to regain their native country by way of
the great continent of South America,
took their paffage home in the long-boat,
through the Streights of Magellan; our
tranfactions during our abode on the
ifland have been related by him in fo
concife a manner as to leave many par-

2   ticulars

ticulars unnoticed, and others touched fo
flightly, that they appear evidently to
have been put together with the purpofe
of juftifying thofe proceedings which
could not be confidered in any other light
than that of direct mutiny. Accordingly, we find that the main fubftance
of his Journal is employed in fcrutini-
zing the conduct of captain Cheap, and
fetting forth the conferences which
paffed between him and the feceders,
relative to the way and meafures they
were to take for their return home. I
have, therefore, taken fome pains to re-
view thofe early paffages of the unfortunate fcene I am to reprefent, and to enter into a detail, without which no found
judgment can be formed of any difputed
point, efpecially when it has been carried fo far as to end in perfonal refent-
ment. When contefts and diffenfions
fhall be found to have gone that length,
it will be obvious to every reader, why a
licentious

licentious crew fhould hearken to any factious leader rather than to the folidity of their captain's advice, who made it evident to every unprejudiced under-ftanding, that their faireft chance for fafety and a better fortune, was to proceed with the long boat till they fhould make prize of fome veffel of the enemy, and thereby be enabled to bring to the commodore a fupply of ftout fellows to affift in his conquefts, and fhare in the honour and rewards.

And yet it is but juftice even to this ungovernable herd to explain, that though I have faid above they appeared in the light of mutineers, they were not actually fuch in the eye of the law; for till a fubfequent act, made, indeed, on this occafion, the pay of a fhip's crew ceafed immediately upon her wreck, and confequently the officers authority and command.

Having

viii PREFACE.

Having explained the foregoing particulars, I hope I may flatter myfelf
there are few things in the following
fheets, which will not be readily underftood by the greateft part of my readers;
therefore I will not detain them any
longer.

T H E

THE

NARRATIVE

OF THE HONOURABLE

JOHN BYRON.

THE equipment and deftination of the fquadron fitted out in the year 1740, of which commodore Anfon had the command, being fufficiently known from the ample and well-penned relation of it under his direction, I fhall recite no particulars that are to be found in that work. But it may be neceffary, for the better underftanding the difaftrous fate of the Wager, the fubject of the following fheets, to repeat the remark, that a

B   ftrange

ftrange infatuation feemed to prevail in
the whole conduct of this embarkation.
For though it was unaccountably detained till the feafon for its failing
was paft, no proper ufe was made of
that time, which fhould have been
employed in providing a fuitable force
of failors and foldiery ; nor was there
a due attention given to other requifites
for fo peculiar and extenfive a deftination.

This neglect not only rendered the
expedition abortive in its principal object, but moft materially affected the
condition of each particular fhip ; and
none fo fatally as the Wager, who being
an old Indiaman bought into the fervice upon this occafion, was now fitted
out as a man of war, but being made
to ferve as a ftore-fhip, was deeply
laden with all kinds of careening geer,
military and other ftores, for the ufe of
the other fhips ; and, what is more,
crowded with bale goods, and encumber-
ed

ed with merchandize. A ship of this quality and condition could not be expected to work with that readiness and ease which was necessary for her security and preservation in those heavy seas with which she was to encounter. Her crew consisted of men pressed from long voyages to be sent upon a distant and hazardous service: on the other hand, all her land-forces were no more than a poor detachment of infirm and decrepid invalids from Chelsea hospital, desponding under the apprehensions of a long voyage. It is not then to be wondered that captain Kid, under whose command this ship sailed out of the port, should in his last moments presage her ill success, though nothing very material happened during his command.

At his death he was succeeded by captain Cheap, who still, without any accident, kept company with the squadron till we had almost gained the

southern-

southernmoft mouth of Straits Le Maire ;
when, being the fternmoft fhip, we were,
by the fudden fhifting of the wind to
the fouthward and the turn of the tide,
very near being wrecked upon the rocks
of Staten Land ; which, notwithftanding,
having weathered, contrary to the expectation of the reft of the fquadron, we endeavoured all in our power to make up
our loft way and regain our ftation. This
we effected, and proceeded in our voyage,
keeping company with the reft of the
fhips for fome time ; when, by a great
roll of a hollow fea, we carried away
our mizen maft, all the chain-plates to
windward being broken. Soon after,
hard gales at weft coming on with a
prodigious fwell, there broke a heavy fea
in upon the fhip, which ftove our boats,
and filled us for fome time.

Thefe accidents were the more dif-
heartening, as our carpenter was on
board the Gloucefter, and detained there

by

by the inceffant tempeftuous weather, and fea impracticable for boats. In a few days he returned, and fupplied the lofs of the mizen-maft by a lower ftudding-fail boom ; but this expedient, together with the patching up of our rigging, was a poor temporary relief to us. We were foon obliged to cut away our beft bower anchor to eafe the fore-maft, the fhrouds and chain-plates of which were all broken, and the fhip in all parts in a moft crazy condition.

Thus fhattered and difabled, a fingle fhip (for we had now loft fight of our fquadron) we had the additional mortification to find ourfelves bearing for the land on a lee-fhore; having thus far perfevered in the courfe we held, from an error in conjecture: for the weather was unfavourable for obfervation, and there are no charts of that part of the coaft. When thofe officers who firft perceived their miftake, endeavoured to perfuade the

captain

captain to alter his courfe, and bear away, for the greater furety, to the weftward, he perfifted in making directly, as he thought, for the ifland of Socoro ; and to fuch as dared from time to time to deliver their doubts of being entangled with the land ftretching to the weftward, he replied, that he thought himfelf in no cafe at liberty to deviate from his orders ; and that the abfence of his fhip from the firft place of rendezvous, would entirely fruftrate the whole fquadron in the firft object of their attack, and poffibly decide upon the fortune of the whole expedition. For the better underftanding the force of his reafoning, it is neceffary to explain, that the ifland of Socoro is in the neighbourhood of Baldivia ; the capture of which place could not be effected without the junction of that fhip which carried the ordnance and military ftores.

The

The knowledge of the great importance of giving so early and unexpected a blow to the Spaniards, determined the captain to make the shortest way to the point in view; and that rigid adherence to orders from which he thought himself in no case at liberty to depart, begot in him a stubborn defiance of all difficulties, and took away from him those apprehensions, which so justly alarmed all such as, from an ignorance of the orders, had nothing present to their minds but the dangers of a lee-shore *.

---

* Captain Cheap has been suspected of a design of going on the Spanish coast without the commodore; but no part of his conduct seems to authorise, in the least, such a suspicion. The author who brings this heavy charge against him, is equally mistaken in imagining that captain Cheap had not instructions to sail to this island, and that the commodore did neither go nor send thither, to inform himself if any of the squadron were there. This appears from the orders delivered to the captains of the squadron, the day before they sailed from St. Catherine's (L. Anson's Voyage, B. I. C. 6.); from the orders of the council of war held on board the Centurion, in the bay of St. Julian

We had for fome time been fenfible
of our approach to the land, from no
other tokens than thofe of weeds and
birds, which are the ufual indications
of nearing the coaft ; but at length we
had an imperfect view of an eminence,
which we conjectured to be one of the
mountains of the Cordilleras. This,
however, was not fo diftinctly feen but
that many conceived it to be the effect
of imagination : but if the captain
was perfuaded of the nearnefs of our
danger, it was now too late to remedy
it ; for at this time the ftraps of the fore
jeer blocks breaking, the fore-yard came
down ; and the greateft part of the men
being difabled through fatigue and ficknefs, it was fome time before it could

(C. 7.); and from the conduct of the commodore (C. 10.)
who cruized (with the utmoft hazard) more than a fortnight off the ifle of Socoro, and along the coaft in its
neighbourhood. It was the fecond rendezvous at Baldivia,
and not that at Socoro, that the commodore was forced by
neceffity to neglect.

be

be got up again. The few hands who were employed in this bufinefs now plainly faw the land on the larboard beam, bearing N. W. upon which the fhip was driving bodily. Orders were then given immediately by the captain to fway the fore-yard up, and fet the fore-fail; which done, we wore fhip with her head to the fouthward, and endeavoured to crowd her off from the land : but the weather, from being exceeding tempeftuous, blowing now a perfect hurricane, and right in upon the fhore, rendered our endeavours (for we were now only twelve hands fit for duty) intirely fruitlefs. The night came on, dreadful beyond defcription, in which, attempting to throw out our topfails to claw off the fhore, they were immediately blown from the yards.

In the morning, about four o'clock, the fhip ftruck. The fhock we received upon this occafion, though very great,

being

being not unlike a blow of a heavy
fea, fuch as in the feries of preceding
ftorms we had often experienced, was
taken for the fame ; but we were foon
undeceived by her ftriking again more
violently than before, which laid her
upon her beam ends, the fea making a
fair breach over her. Every perfon that
now could ftir was prefently upon the
quarter deck ; and many even of thofe
were alert upon this occafion, that
had not fhewed their faces upon deck
for above two months before : feveral
poor wretches, who were in the laft ftage
of the fcurvy, and who could not get
out of their hammocks, were immediately drowned.

In this dreadful fituation fhe lay for
fome little time, every foul on board
looking upon the prefent minute as his
laft ; for there was nothing to be feen
but breakers all around us. However,
a mountainous fea hove her off from
thence ;

thence; but fhe prefently ftruck again, and broke her tiller. In this terrifying and critical juncture, to have obferved all the various modes of horror operating according to the feveral characters and complexions amongft us, it was neceffary that the obferver himfelf fhould have been free from all impreffions of danger. Inftances there were, however, of behaviour fo very remarkable, they could not efcape the notice of any one who was not intirely bereaved of his fenfes; for fome were in this condition to all intents and purpofes; particularly one, in the ravings defpair brought upon him, was feen ftalking about the deck, flourifhing a cutlafs over his head, and calling himfelf king of the country, and ftriking every body he came near, till his companions, feeing no other fecurity againft his tyranny, knocked him down. Some, reduced before by long ficknefs and the fcurvy,

became

became on this occafion as it were pe-
trified and bereaved of all fenfe, like in-
animate logs, and were bandied to and
fro by the jerks and rolls of the fhip,
without exerting any efforts to help
themfelves. So terrible was the fcene
of foaming breakers around us, that
one of the braveft men we had could
not help expreffing his difmay at it,
faying it was too fhocking a fight to
bear; and would have thrown himfelf
over the rails of the quarter-deck into
the fea, had he not been prevented: but
at the fame time there were not wanting
thofe who preferved a prefence of mind
truly heroic. The man at the helm,
though both rudder and tiller were gone,
kept his ftation; and being afked by one
of the officers, if the fhip would fteer or
not, firft took his time to make trial by the
wheel, and then anfwered with as much
refpect and coolnefs as if the fhip had
been in the greateft fafety; and immediately

ately after applied himſelf with his uſual ſerenity, to his duty, perſuaded it did not become him to deſert it as long as the ſhip kept together. Mr. Jones, mate, who now ſurvives not only this wreck, but that of the Litchfield man of war upon the coaſt of Barbary, at the time when the ſhip was in the moſt imminent danger, not only ſhewed himſelf undaunted, but endeavoured to inſpire the ſame reſolution in the men; ſaying, " My friends, let us not be diſcouraged: did you never ſee a ſhip amongſt breakers before? Let us try to puſh her through them. Come, lend a hand; here is a ſheet, and here is a brace; lay hold; I don't doubt but we may ſtick her yet near enough to the land to ſave our lives." This had ſo good an effect, that many who before were half dead, ſeemed active again, and now went to work in earneſt. This Mr. Jones did purely to keep up the ſpirits of the

the people as long as poffible; for he often faid afterwards, he thought there was not the leaft chance of a fingle man's being faved. We now run in between an opening of the breakers, fteering by the fheets and braces, when providentially we ftuck faft between two great rocks ; that to windward fheltering us in fome meafure from the violence of the fea. We immediately cut away the main and foremaft; but the fhip kept beating in fuch a manner, that we imagined fhe could hold together but a very little while. The day now broke, and the weather, that had been extremely thick, cleared away for a few moments, and gave us a glimpfe of the land not far from us. We now thought of nothing but faving our lives. To get the boats out, as our mafts were gone, was a work of fome time ; which when accomplifhed, many were ready to jump into the firft, by which means they nar-

rowly

rowly efcaped perifhing before they reached the fhore. I now went to captain Cheap (who had the misfortune to diflocate his fhoulder by a fall the day before, as he was going forward to get the fore-yard fwayed up), and afked him if he would not go on fhore; but he told me, as he had done before, that he would be the laft to leave the fhip; and he ordered me to affift in getting the men out as foon as poffible. I had been with him very often from the time the fhip firft ftruck, as he defired I would, to acquaint him with every thing that paffed; and I particularly remarked, that he gave his orders at that time with as much coolnefs as ever he had done during the former part of the voyage.

The fcene was now greatly changed; for many who but a few minutes before had fhewn the ftrongeft figns of defpair, and were on their knees praying for mercy, imagining they

were

were now not in that immediate danger,
grew very riotous, broke open every
cheft and box that was at hand, ftove
in the heads of cafks of brandy and
wine as they were born up to the hatch-
ways, and got fo drunk, that feveral of
them were drowned on board, and lay
floating about the decks for fome days
after. Before I left the fhip, I went
down to my cheft, which was at the
bulk-head of the wardroom, in order to
fave fome little matters, if poffible ; but
whilft I was there the fhip thumped with
fuch violence, and the water came in fo
faft, that I was forced to get upon the
quarter-deck again, without faving a
fingle rag but what was upon my back.
The boatfwain and fome of the people
would not leave the fhip fo long as there
was any liquor to be got at ; upon which
captain Cheap fuffered himfelf to be
helped out of his bed, put into the boat,
and carried on fhore.

It

It is natural to think, that to men thus upon the point of perifhing by fhipwreck, the getting to land was the higheft attainment of their wifhes; undoubtedly it was a defirable event; yet, all things confidered, our condition was but little mended by the change. Which ever way we looked, a fcene of horror prefented itfelf : on one fide, the wreck (in which was all that we had in the world to fupport and fubfift us), together with a boifterous fea, prefented us with the moft dreary profpect; on the other, the land did not wear a much more favourable appearance : defolate and barren, without fign of culture, we could hope to receive little other benefit from it than the prefervation it afforded us from the fea. It muft be confeffed this was a great and merciful deliverance from immediate deftruction; but then we had wet, cold, and hunger, to ftruggle with, and no vifible remedy

C   againft

againft any of thefe evils. Exerting ourfelves, however, though faint, benumbed,
and almoft helplefs, to find fome wretched covert againft the extreme inclemency
of the weather, we difcovered an Indian
hut, at a fmall diftance from the beach,
within a wood, in which as many as
poffible, without diftinction, crouded
themfelves, the night coming on exceedingly tempeftuous and rainy. But here
our fituation was fuch as to exclude all reft
and refrefhment by fleep from moft of
us ; for befides that we preffed upon one
another extremely, we were not without
our alarms and apprehenfions of being
attacked by the Indians, from a difcovery we made of fome of their lances
and other arms in our hut ; and our uncertainty of their ftrength and difpofition gave alarm to our imagination,
and kept us in continual anxiety.

In this miferable hovel, one of our
company, a lieutenant of invalids, died
this

this night; and of thofe who for want
of room took fhelter under a great tree,
which ftood them in very little ftead, two
more perifhed by the feverity of that
cold and rainy night. In the morning,
the calls of hunger, which had been
hitherto fuppreffed by our attention to
more immediate dangers and difficulties,
were now become too importunate to be
refifted. We had moft of us fafted
eight and forty hours, fome more; it
was time, therefore, to make enquiry
among ourfelves what ftore of fuftenance had been brought from the wreck
by the providence of fome, and what
could be procured on the ifland by the
induftry of others : but the produce of
the one amounted to no more than two
or three pounds of bifcuit duft referved
in a bag; and all the fuccefs of thofe
who ventured abroad, the weather being
ftill exceedingly bad, was to kill one fea-
gull and pick fome wild fellery. Thefe,

therefore,

therefore, were immediately put into a pot, with the addition of a large quantity of water, and made into a kind of foup, of which each partook as far as it would go; but we had no fooner thrown this down than we were feized with the moft painful ficknefs at our ftomachs, violent reachings, fwoonings, and other fymptoms of being poifoned. This was imputed to various caufes, but in general to the herbs we made ufe of, in the nature and quality of which we fancied ourfelves miftaken; but a little further enquiry let us into the real occafion of it, which was no other than this: the bifcuit duft was the fweepings of the bread-room, but the bag in which they were put had been a tobacco bag; the contents of which not being intirely taken out, what remained mixed with the bifcuit-duft, and proved a ftrong emetic.

We

We were in all about a hundred and forty who had got to fhore; but fome few remained ftill on board, detained either by drunkennefs, or a view of pillaging the wreck, among which was the boatfwain. Thefe were vifited by an officer in the yawl, who was to endeavour to prevail upon them to join the reft; but finding them in the greateft diforder, and difpofed to mutiny, he was obliged to defift from his purpofe and return without them. Though we were very defirous, and our neceffities required that we fhould take fome furvey of the land we were upon; yet being ftrongly prepoffeffed that the favages were retired but fome little diftance from us, and waited to fee us divided, our parties did not make this day, any great excurfions from the hut; but as far as we went, we found it very moraffy and unpromifing. The fpot which we occupied was a bay formed by hilly promontories; that to

the

the north fo exceeding fteep, that in order to afcend it (for there was no going
round, the bottom being wafhed by the
fea) we were at the labour of cutting
fteps. This, which we called Mount
Mifery, was of ufe to us in taking fome
obfervations afterwards, when the weather would permit: the fouthern pro-
montory was not fo inacceffible. Beyond this I, with fome others, having
reached another bay, found driven afhore
fome parts of the wreck, but no kind of
provifion : nor did we meet with any
fhell-fifh, which we were chiefly in
fearch of. We therefore returned to the
reft, and for that day made no other repaft than what the wild fellery afforded
us. The enfuing night proved exceedingly tempeftuous ; and, the fea running
very high, threatened thofe on board
with immediate deftruction by the part-
ing of the wreck. They then were
as follicitous to get afhore, as they
were

were before obftinate in refufing the affiftance we fent them; and when they
found the boat did not come to their relief at the inftant they expected it,
without confidering how impracticable
a thing it was to fend it them in fuch a
fea, they fired one of the quarter-deck
guns at the hut; the ball of which did
but juft pafs over the covering of it, and
was plainly heard by the captain and us
who were within. Another attempt,
therefore, was made to bring thefe mad-
men to land; which, however, by the
violence of the fea, and other impediments,
occafioned by the maft that lay along-
fide, proved ineffectual. This unavoid-
able delay made the people on board
outrageous: they fell to beating every
thing to pieces that fell in the way;
and, carrying their intemperance to the
greateft excefs, broke open chefts and
cabbins for plunder that could be of no
ufe to them: and fo earneft were they

in

in this wantonnefs of theft, that one
man had evidently been murdered on
account of fome divifion of the fpoil, or
for the fake of the fhare that fell to him,
having all the marks of a ftrangled
corpfe. One thing in this outrage they
feemed particularly attentive to, which
was, to provide themfelves with arms
and ammunition, in order to fupport them
in putting their mutinous defigns in execution, and afferting their claim to a
lawlefs exemption from the authority
of their officers, which they pretended
muft ceafe with the lofs of the fhip.
But of thefe arms, which we ftood in
great need of, they were foon bereaved,
upon coming afhore, by the refolution
of captain Cheap and lieutenant Hamilton of the marines. Among thefe mutineers which had been left on board, as
I obferved before, was the boatfwain;
who, inftead of exerting the authority he
had over the reft, to keep them within
bounds

bounds as much as poffible, was himfelf
a ringleader in their riot: him, without
refpect to the figure he then made, for he
was in laced cloaths, captain Cheap, by a
blow well laid on with his cane, felled
to the ground. It was fcarce poffible to refrain from laughter at the
whimfical appearance thefe fellows made,
who, having rifled the chefts of the officers beft fuits, had put them on over
their greafy trowfers and dirty checked
fhirts. They were foon ftripped of their
finery, as they had before been obliged
to refign their arms.

The inceffant rains, and exceeding
cold weather in this climate, rendered it
impoffible for us to fubfift long without fhelter; and the hut being much too
little to receive us all, it was neceffary to
fall upon fome expedient, without delay, which might ferve our purpofe:
accordingly the gunner, carpenter, and
fome more, turning the cutter keel upwards,

wards, and fixing it upon props, made no defpicable habitation. Having thus eftablifhed fome fort of fettlement, we had the more leifure to look about us, and to make our refearches with greater accuracy than we had before, after fuch fupplies as the moft defolate coafts are feldom unfurnifhed with. Accordingly we foon provided ourfelves with fome fea-fowl, and found limpets, mufcles, and other fhell-fifh in tolerable abundance ; but this rummaging of the fhore was now becoming extremely irkfome to thofe who had any feeling, by the bodies of our drowned people thrown among the rocks, fome of which were hideous fpectacles, from the mangled condition they were in by the violent furf that drove in upon the coaft. Thefe horrors were overcome by the diftreffes of our people, who were even glad of the occafion of killing the gallinazo (the carrion crow of that country) while

while preying on thefe carcaffes, in order to make a meal of them. But a provifion by no means proportionable to the number of mouths to be fed could, by our utmoft induftry, be acquired from that part of the ifland we had hitherto traverfed : therefore, till we were in a capacity of making more diftant excurfions, the wreck was to be applied to, as often as poffible, for fuch fupplies as could be got out of her. But as this was a very precarious fund in its prefent fituation, and at beft could not laft us long; confidering too that it was very uncertain how long we might be detained upon this ifland ; the ftores and provifion we were fo fortunate as to retrieve, were not only to be dealt out with the moft frugal œconomy, but a fufficient quantity, if poffible, laid by, to fit us out, whenever we could agree upon any method of tranfporting ourfelves from this dreary fpot. The difficulties we had to

encounter

encounter in thefe vifits to the wreck, cannot be eafily defcribed; for no part of it being above water except the quarter-deck and part of the fore-caftle, we were ufually obliged to purchafe fuch things as were within reach, by means of large hooks faftened to poles, in which bufi-nefs we were much incommoded by the dead bodies floating between decks. In order to fecure what we thus got in a manner to anfwer the ends and purpofes above-mentioned, captain Cheap ordered a ftore-tent to be erected near his hut, as a repofitory, from which no-thing was to be dealt out, but in the meafure and proportion agreed upon by the officers; and though it was very hard upon us petty officers, who were fatigued with hunting all day in queft of food, to defend this tent from invafion by night, no other means could be devifed for this purpofe fo effectual as the committing this charge to our care; and we were ac-

cordingly

cordingly ordered to divide the task
equally between us. Yet, notwithstand-
ing our utmost vigilance and care, frequent robberies were committed upon
our truft, the tent being acceffible in more
than one place. And one night, when
I had the watch, hearing a ftir within,
I came unawares upon the thief, and
prefenting a piftol to his breaft, obliged
him to fubmit to be tied up to a poft, till
I had an opportunity of fecuring him
more effectually. Depredations continued to be made on our referved ftock,
notwithftanding the great hazard attending fuch attempts; for our common fafety
made it neceffary to punifh them with
the utmoft rigour. This will not be
wondered at, when it is known how
little the allowance which might confiftently be difpenfed from thence, was proportionable to our common exigencies;
fo that our daily and nightly task of
roving after food, was not in the leaft
relaxed

relaxed thereby ; and all put together
was fo far from anfwering our neceffities, that many at this time perifhed
with hunger. A boy, when no other
eatables could be found, having picked
up the liver of one of the drowned men
(whofe carcafe had been torn to pieces
by the force with which the fea drove
it among the rocks) was with difficulty
withheld from making a meal of it. The
men were fo affiduous in their refearch
after the few things which drove from the
wreck, that in order to have no fharers
of their good fortune, they examined
the fhore no lefs by night than by day ;
fo that many of thofe who were lefs
alert, or not fo fortunate as their neigh-
bours, perifhed with hunger, or were
driven to the laft extremity. It muft
be obferved that on the 14th of May we
were caft away, and it was not till the
twenty-fifth of this month, that provifion
was ferved regularly from the ftore-tent.

The

The land we were now fettled upon was about 90 leagues to the northward of the weftern mouth of the ftreights of Magellan, in the latitude of between 47 and 48° fouth, from whence we could plainly fee the Cordilleras; and by two Lagoons on the north and fouth of us, ftretching towards thofe mountains, we conjectured it was an ifland. But as yet we had no means of informing ourfelves perfectly, whether it was an ifland or the main; for befides that the inland parts at little diftance from us feemed impracticable, from the exceeding great thicknefs of the wood, we had hitherto been in fuch confufion and want (each finding full employment for his time, in fcraping together a wretched fubfiftence, and providing fhelter againft the cold and rain) that no party could be formed to go upon difcoveries. The climate and feafon too were utterly unfavourable to adventurers, and the coaft, as far as our

eye

eye could ftretch feaward, a fcene of fuch difmal breakers as would difcourage the moft daring from making attempts in fmall boats. Nor were we affifted in our enquiries by any obfervation that could be made from that eminence we called Mount Mifery, toward land, our profpect that way being intercepted by ftill higher hills and lofty woods : we had therefore no other expedient, by means of which to come at this know-ledge, but by fitting out one of our fhip's boats upon fome difcovery, to inform us of our fituation. Our long boat was ftill on board the wreck ; therefore a number of hands were now difpatched to cut the gunwale of the fhip, in order to get her out. Whilft we were em-ployed in this bufinefs, there appeared three canoes of Indians paddling towards us : they had come round the point from the fouthern Lagoons. It was fome time before we could prevail upon them

to

to lay afide their fears and approach us; which at length they were induced to do by the figns of friendfhip we made them, and by fhewing fome bale-goods, which they accepted, and fuffered themfelves to be conducted to the captain, who made them, likewife, fome prefents. They were ftrangely affected with the novelty thereof; but chiefly when fhewn the looking-glafs, in which the beholder could not conceive it to be his own face that was reprefented, but that of fome other behind it, which he therefore went round to the back of the glafs to find out.

Thefe people were of a fmall ftature, very fwarthy, having long, black, coarfe hair, hanging over their faces. It was evident, from their great furprife, and every part of their behaviour, as well as their not having one thing in their pof-feffion which could be derived from white people, that they had never feen fuch. Their cloathing was nothing but a

bit

bit of fome beaft's fkin about their waifts, and fomething woven from feathers over the fhoulders; and as they uttered no word of any language we had ever heard, nor had any method of making themfelves underftood, we prefumed they could have had no intercourfe with Europeans. Thefe favages, who upon their departure left us a few mufcles, returned in two days, and furprifed us by bringing three fheep. From whence they could procure thefe animals in a part of the world fo diftant from any Spanifh fettlement, cut off from all communication with the Spaniards by an inacceffible coaft and unprofitable country, is difficult to conceive. Certain it is, that we faw no fuch creatures, nor ever heard of any fuch, from the Streights of Magellan, till we got into the neighbourhood of Chiloe: it muft be by fome ftrange accident that thefe creatures came into their poffeffion; but what that was,

we

we never could learn from them. At this interview we bartered with them for a dog or two, which we roafted and eat. In a few days after, they made us another vifit, and bringing their wives with them, took up their abode with us for fome days ; then again left us.

Whenever the weather permitted, which was now grown fomething drier, but exceeding cold, we employed our-felves about the wreck, from which we had, at fundry times, recovered feveral articles of provifion and liquor : thefe were depofited in the ftore-tent. Ill-humour and difcontent, from the diffi-culties we laboured under in procuring fubfiftence, and the little profpect there was of any amendment in our condition, was now breaking out apace. In fome it fhewed itfelf by a feparation of fettle-ment and habitation ; in others, by a refo-lution of leaving the captain entirely, and making a wild journey by them-

felves,

felves, without determining upon any plan whatever. For my own part, feeing it was the fafhion, and liking none of their parties, I built a little hut juft big enough for myfelf and a poor Indian dog I found in the woods, who could fhift for himfelf along fhore, at low water, by getting limpets. This creature grew fo fond of me and faithful, that he would fuffer nobody to come near the hut without biting them. Befides thofe feceders I mentioned, fome laid a fcheme of deferting us entirely : thefe were in number ten ; the greateft part of them a moft defperate and abandoned crew, who, to ftrike a notable ftroke before they went off, placed half a barrel of gunpowder clofe to the captain's hut, laid a train to it, and were juft preparing to perpetrate their wicked defign of blowing up their commander, when they were with diffi-culty diffuaded from it by one who had fome bowels and remorfe of confcience

8   left

left in him. Thefe wretches, after ram-
bling fome time in the woods, and finding it impracticable to get off, for they
were then convinced that we were not
upon the main, as they had imagined
when they firft left us, but upon an
ifland within four or five leagues of it,
returned and fettled about a league from
us ; however, they were ftill determined,
as foon as they could procure craft fit
for their purpofe, to get to the main.
But before they could effect this, we
found means to prevail upon the ar-
mourer and one of the carpenter's
crew, two very ufeful men to us, who
had imprudently joined them, to come
over again to their duty. The reft, (one
or two excepted) having built a punt,
and converted the hull of one of the
fhip's mafts into a canoe, went away
up one of the Lagoons, and never were
heard of more.

Thefe being a defperate and factious

D 3   fet,

fet, did not diftrefs us much by their departure, but rather added to our future
fecurity : one in particular, James Mit-
chell by name, we had all the reafon in
the world to think had committed no lefs
than two murders fince the lofs of our
fhip ; one on the perfon found ftrangled
on board, another on the body of a man
whom we difcovered among fome bufhes
upon Mount Mifery, ftabbed in feveral
places, and fhockingly mangled. This
diminution of our numbers was fucceeded by an unfortunate accident much
more affecting in its confequences, I
mean the death of Mr. Cozens, midfhip-
man ; in relating which with the neceffary impartiality and exactnefs, I think
myfelf obliged to be more than ordinary
particular. Having one day, among other
things, got a cafk of peafe out of the
wreck, about which I was almoft conftantly employed, I brought it to fhore
in the yawl ; when having landed
it,

it, the captain came down upon the beach,
and bid me to go up to some of the tents
and order hands to come down and roll it
up ; but finding none except Mr. Cozens,
I delivered him the orders, who immediately came down to the captain, where
I left them when I returned to the wreck.
Upon my coming on shore again, I
found that Mr. Cozens was put under
confinement by the captain, for being
drunk and giving him abusive language;
however, he was soon after released.   A
day or two after he had some dispute with
the surgeon, and came to blows : all these
things incensed the captain greatly
against him.   I believe this unfortunate
man was kept warm with liquor, and set
on by some ill-designing persons ; for,
when sober, I never knew a better na-
tured man, or one more inoffensive.
Some little time after, at the hour of
serving provisions, Mr. Cozens was at the
store tent ; and having, it seems, lately

had

had a quarrel with the purfer; and now fome words arifing between them, the latter told him he was come to mutiny; and without any further ceremony fired a piftol at his head, which narrowly miffed him. The captain, hearing the report of the piftol, and perhaps the purfer's words, that Cozens was come to mutiny, ran out of his hut with a cocked piftol in his hand, and, without afking any queftions, immediately fhot him through the head. I was at this time in my hut, as the weather was extremely bad ; but running out upon the alarm of this firing, the firft thing I faw was Mr. Cozens on the ground, weltering in his blood: he was fenfible, and took me by the hand, as he did feveral others, fhaking his head, as if he meant to take leave of us. If Mr. Cozens' behaviour to his captain was indecent and provoking, the captain's, on the other hand, was rafh and hafty: if the firft was wanting in

that

that refpect and obfervance which is due
from a petty officer to his commander,
the latter was ftill more unadvifed in the
method he took for the enforcement of
his authority ; of which, indeed, he was
jealous to the laft degree, and which he
faw daily declining, and ready to be
trampled upon. His miftaken appre-
henfion of a mutinous defign in Mr. Cozens, the fole motive of this rafh action,
was fo far from anfwering the end he
propofed by it, that the men, who before
were much diffatisfied and uneafy, were
by this unfortunate ftep thrown almoft
into open fedition and revolt. It was
evident that the people, who ran out of
their tents, alarmed by the report of fire-
arms, though they difguifed their real
fentiments for the prefent, were extremely
affected at this cataftrophe of Mr. Cozens
(for he was greatly beloved by them):
their minds were now exafperated, and
it was to be apprehended, that their re-
fentment,

fentment, which was fmothered for the prefent, would fhortly fhew itfelf in fome defperate enterprife. The unhappy victim, who lay weltering in his blood on the ground before them, feemed to abforb their whole attention; the eyes of all were fixed upon him; and vifible marks of the deepeft concern appeared in the countenances of the fpectators. The perfuafion the captain was under, at the time he fhot Mr. Cozens, that his intentions were mutinous, together with a jealoufy of the diminution of his authority, occafioned alfo his behaving with lefs compaffion and tendernefs towards him afterwards than was confiftent with the unhappy condition of the poor fufferer: for when it was begged as a favour by his mefs-mates, that Mr. Cozens might be removed to their tent, though a neceffary thing in his dangerous fituation, yet it was not permitted; but the poor wretch was fuffered to languifh on

I   the

the ground fome days, with no other covering than a bit of canvas thrown over
fome bufhes, where he died. But to
return to our ftory : the captain, addref-
fing himfelf to the people thus affem-
bled, told them, that it was his refolution to maintain his command over
them as ufual, which ftill remained in as
much force as ever ; and then ordered
them all to return to their refpective tents,
with which order they inftantly com-
plied. Now we had faved the long-boat
from the wreck, and got it in our poffeffion, there was nothing that feemed
fo neceffary towards the advancing
our delivery from this defolate place,
as the new modelling this veffel fo as to
have room for all thofe who were inclined
to go off in her, and to put her in a condition to bear the ftormy feas we muft of
courfe encounter. We therefore hauled
her up, and having placed her upon
blocks, fawed her in two, in order to
lengthen

lengthen her about twelve feet by the keel. For this purpofe, all thofe who could be fpared from the more immediate tafk of procuring fubfiftence, were employed in fitting and fhaping timber as the carpenter directed them; I fay, in procuring fubfiftence, becaufe the weather lately having been very tempeftuous, and the wreck working much, had difgorged a great part of her contents, which were every where difperfed about the fhore.

We now fent frequent parties up the Lagoons, which fometimes fucceeded in getting fome fea-fowl for us. The Indians appearing again in the offing, we put off our yawl, in order to fruftrate any defign they might have of going up the Lagoon towards the deferters, who would have availed themfelves of fome of their canoes to have got upon the main. Having conducted them in, we found that their intention was to fettle among us, for they had brought their

wives

wives and children with them, in all about fifty perfons, who immediately fet about building themfelves wigwams, and feemed much reconciled to our company ; and, could we have entertained them as we ought, they would have been of great affiftance to us, who were yet extremely put to it to fubfift ourfelves; being a hundred in number ; but the men, now fubject to little or no controul, endeavoured to feduce their wives, which gave the Indians fuch offence, that in a fhort time they found means to depart, taking every thing along with them ; and we being fenfible of the caufe, never expected to fee them return again. The carpenter having made fome progrefs in his work upon the long-boat, in which he was enabled to proceed tolerably, by the tools and other articles of his bufi-nefs retrieved from the wreck, the men began to think of the courfe they fhould take to get home ; or rather, having bor-
rowed

rowed Sir John Narborough's Voyage of captain Cheap, by the application of Mr. Bulkely, which book he faw me reading one day in my tent, they, immediately upon perufing it, concluded upon making their voyage home by the Streights of Magellan. This plan was propofed to the captain, who by no means approved of it, his defign being to go northwards, with a view of feizing a fhip of the enemy's, by which means he might join the commodore: at prefent, therefore, here it refted. But the men were in high fpirits from the profpect they had of getting off in the long-boat, overlooking all the difficulties and hazards of a voyage almoft impracticable, and carefling the carpenter, who indeed was an excellent workman, and deferved all the encouragement they could give him. The Indians having left us, and the weather continuing tempeftuous and rainy, the diftreffes of the people, for want of food, became

became infupportable. Our number, which was at firft 145, was now reduced to 100, and chiefly by famine, which put the reft upon all fhifts and devices to fupport themfelves. One day, when I was at home in my hut with my Indian dog, a party came to my door, and told me their neceffities were fuch, that they muft eat the creature or ftarve. Though their plea was urgent, I could not help ufing fome arguments to endeavour to diffuade them from killing him, as his faithful fervices and fondnefs deferved it at my hands; but, without weighing my arguments, they took him away by force and killed him; upon which, thinking that I had at leaft as good a right to a fhare as the reft, I fat down with them, and partook of their repaft. Three weeks after that I was glad to make a meal of his paws and fkin, which, upon recollecting the fpot where they had killed him, I found

thrown

thrown afide and rotten. The preffing calls of hunger drove our men to their wits end, and put them upon a variety of devices to fatisfy it. Among the ingenious this way, one Phips, a boatfwain's mate, having got a water puncheon, fcuttled it; then lafhing two logs, one on each fide, fet out in queft of adventures in this extraordinary and original piece of imbarkation. By this means he would frequently, when all the reft were ftarving, provide himfelf with wild-fowl ; and it muft have been very bad weather indeed which could deter him from putting out to fea when his occafions required. Sometimes he would venture far out in the offing, and be abfent the whole day : at laft, it was his misfortune, at a great diftance from fhore, to be overfet by a heavy fea ; but being near a rock, though no fwimmer, he managed fo as to fcramble to it, and with great difficulty afcended it : there he remained two

days

with very little hopes of any relief, for
he was too far off to be feen from fhore;
but fortunately a boat, having put off
and gone in queft of wild-fowl that way,
difcovered him making fuch fignals as
he was able, and brought him back to
the ifland. But this accident did not fo
difcourage him but that foon after, having procured an ox's hide, ufed on board
for fifting powder, and called a gunner's
hide, by the affiftance of fome hoops he
formed fomething like a canoe, in which
he made feveral fuccefsful voyages.
When the weather would permit us, we
feldom failed of getting fome wild-fowl,
though never in any plenty, by putting
off with our boats; but this moft inhofpitable climate is not only deprived of
the fun for the moft part, by a thick,
rainy atmofphere, but is alfo vifited by
almoft inceffant tempefts. It muft be
confeffed, we reaped fome benefit from
thefe hard gales and overgrown feas,

E which

which drove feveral things afhore; but there was no dependance on fuch accidental relief; and we were always alert to avail ourfelves of every interval of fair weather, though fo little to be depended on, that we were often unexpectedly and to our peril overtaken by a fudden change. In one of our excurfions I, with two more, in a wretched punt of our own making, had no fooner landed at our ftation upon a high rock, than the punt was driven loofe by a fudden fquall; and had not one of the men, at the rifk of his life, jumped into the fea and fwam on board her, we muft in all probability have perifhed; for we were more than three leagues from the ifland at the time. Among the birds we generally fhot, was the painted goofe, whofe plumage is variegated with the moft lively colours; and a bird much larger than a goofe, which we called the racehorfe, from the velocity with which

it

it moved upon the furface of the water, in a fort of half flying, half running motion. But we were not fo fuccefsful in our endeavours by land ; for though we fometimes got pretty far into the woods, we met with very few birds in all our walks. We never faw but three woodcocks, two of which were killed by Mr. Hamilton, and one by myfelf. Thefe, with fome humming-birds, and a large kind of robin redbreaft, were the only feathered inhabitants of this ifland, excepting a fmall bird with two very long feathers in his tail, which was generally feen amongft the rocks, and was fo tame, that I have had them reft upon my fhoulder whilft I have been gathering fhell- fifh. Indeed, we were vifited by many birds of prey, fome very large; but thefe only occafionally, and, as we imagined, allured by fome dead whale in the neighbourhood, which was once feen. However, if we

E 2   were

were fo fortunate as to kill one of them, we thought ourfelves very well off. In one of my walks, feeing a bird of this latter kind upon an eminence, I endeavoured to come upon it unperceived with my gun, by means of the woods which lay at the back of that eminence; but when I had proceeded fo far in the wood as to think I was in a line with it, I heard a growling clofe by me, which made me think it advifable to retire as foon as poffible: the woods were fo gloomy I could fee nothing; but as I retired, this noife followed me clofe till I had got out of them. Some of our men did affure me, that they had feen a very large beaft in the woods; but their defcription of it was too imperfect to be relied upon. The wood here is chiefly of the aromatic kind; the iron wood, a wood of a very deep red hue, and another, of an exceeding bright yellow. All the low fpots are very fwampy; but what

we

we thought ſtrange, upon the ſummits
of the higheſt hills were found beds of
ſhells, a foot or two thick.

The long-boat being near finiſhed,
ſome of our company were ſelected to go
out in the barge, in order to reconnoitre
the coaſt to the ſouthward, which might
aſſiſt us in the navigation we were going upon. This party conſiſted of Mr.
Bulkely, Mr. Jones, the purſer, myſelf,
and ten men. The firſt night, we put
into a good harbour, a few leagues to
the ſouthward of Wager's Iſland; where
finding a large bitch big with puppies,
we regaled upon them. In this expedition we had our uſual bad weather, and
breaking ſeas, which were grown to ſuch
a height the third day, that we were obliged, through diſtreſs, to puſh in at the
firſt inlet we ſaw at hand. This we had
no ſooner entered, than we were pre-
ſented with a view of a fine bay, in
which having ſecured the barge, we

E 3   went

went afhore ; but the weather being very
rainy, and finding nothing to fubfift
upon, we pitched a bell tent, which we
had brought with us, in the wood oppofite to where the barge lay. As this
tent was not large enough to contain us all, I propofed to four of the
people, to go to the end of the bay,
about two miles diftant from the bell
tent, to occupy the fkeleton of an old
Indian wigwam, which I had difcovered
in a walk that way upon our firft landing. This we covered to windward
with fea-weed ; and lighting a fire, laid
ourfelves down, in hopes of finding a
remedy for our hunger in fleep ; but
we had not long compofed ourfelves before one of our company was difturbed by the blowing of fome animal
at his face, and upon opening his eyes,
was not a little aftonifhed to fee, by the
glimmering of the fire, a large beaft
ftanding over him. He had prefence of
mind

mind enough to fnatch a brand from the fire, which was now very low, and thruft it at the nofe of the animal, who thereupon made off: this done, the man awoke us, and related, with horror in his countenance, the narrow efcape he had of being devoured. But though we were under no fmall apprehenfions of another vifit from this animal, yet our fatigue and heavinefs was greater than our fears ; and we once more compofed ourfelves to reft, and flept the remainder of the night without any further difturbance. In the morning, we were not a little anxious to know how our companions had fared ; and this anxiety was increafed upon tracing the footfteps of the beaft in the fand, in a direction towards the bell tent. The impreffion was deep and plain, of a large round foot well furnifhed with claws. Upon our acquainting the people in the tent with the circumftances of our

E 4   ftory,

ftory, we found that they too, had
been vifited by the fame unwelcome
gueft, which they had driven away by
much the fame expedient. We now returned from this cruife, with a ftrong
gale, to Wager's ifland; having found it
impracticable to make farther difcoveries
in the barge, on fo dangerous a coaft,
and in fuch heavy feas. Here we foon
difcovered, by the quarters of dogs
hanging up, that the Indians had
brought a frefh fupply to our market.
Upon enquiry, we found that there had
been fix canoes of them, who, among
other methods of taking fifh, had taught
their dogs to drive the fifh into a corner
of fome pond, or lake, from whence
they were eafily taken out, by the fkill
and addrefs of thefe favages. The old
cabal, during our abfence, had been frequently revived; the debates of which
generally ended in riot and drunkennefs.
This cabal was chiefly held in a large
tent,

tent, which the people belonging to it
had taken fome pains to make fnug and
convenient, and lined with bales of
broad cloth driven from the wreck.
Eighteen of the ftouteft fellows of
the fhip's company had poffeffion of
this tent, from whence were difpatched committees to the captain, with
the refolutions they had taken with
regard to their departure ; but oft-
ener for liquor. Their determination
was to go in the long-boat to the fouthward, by the Streights of Magellan ; and
the point they were labouring, was to
prevail upon the captain to accompany
them. But though he had fixed upon a
quite different plan, which was to go to
the northward, yet he thought it politic,
at prefent, feemingly to acquiefce with
them, in order to keep them quiet.
When they began to ftipulate with him,
that he fhould be under fome reftric-
tions in point of command, and fhould

do

do nothing without confulting his officers, he infifted upon the full exercife of
his authority, as before. This broke
all meafures between them, and they
were from this time determined he
fhould go with them, whether he would
or no. A better pretence they could
not have for effecting this defign, than
the unfortunate affair of Mr. Cozens;
which they therefore made ufe of for
feizing his perfon, and putting him under confinement, in order to bring him
to his trial in England. The long boat
was now launched, and ready for failing,
and all the men embarked, except captain Pemberton, with a party of marines,
who drew them up upon the beach
with intent to conduct captain Cheap
on board; but he was at length perfuaded to defift from this refolution by
Mr. Bulkly. The men too, finding
they were ftraitened for room, and that
their ftock of provifion would not admit

mit of their taking fupernumeraries aboard, were now no lefs ftrenuous for his enlargement, and being left to his option of ftaying behind. Therefore, after having diftributed their fhare in the referved ftock of provifion, which was very fmall, we departed, leaving captain Cheap, Mr. Hamilton of the marines, and the furgeon, upon the ifland. I had all along been in the dark as to the turn this affair would take ; and not in the leaft fufpecting but that it was determined captain Cheap fhould be taken with us, readily embarked under that perfuafion; but when I found that this defign, which was fo ferioufly carried on to the laft, was fuddenly dropped, I was determined, upon the firft opportunity, to leave them ; which was at this inftant impoffible for me to do, the long-boat lying fome diftance off fhore, at anchor. We were in all eighty-one, when we left the ifland, diftributed into the

long-

long-boat, cutter, and barge ; fifty-nine on board the firft, twelve in the fecond, in the laft, ten. It was our purpofe to put into fome harbour, if poffible, every evening, as we were in no condition to keep thofe terrible feas long ; for without other affiftance, our ftock of provivifions was no more than might have been confumed in a few days; our water was chiefly contained in a few powder-barrels ; our flour was to be lengthened out by a mixture of fea-weed ; and our other fupplies depended upon the fuccefs of our guns, and induftry among the rocks. Captain Pemberton having brought on board his men, we weighed ; but by a fudden fquall of wind having fplit our forefail, we with difficulty cleared the rocks, by means of our boats, bore away for a fandy bay, on the fouth fide of the Lagoon, and anchored in ten fathom. The next morning we got under way ; but it blowing hard at W. by N.

with

with a great fwell, put into a fmall bay again, well fheltered by a ledge of rocks without us. At this time, it was thought neceffary to fend the barge away back to Cheap's bay, for fome fpare canvas, which was imagined would be foon wanted. I thought this a good opportunity of returning, and therefore made one with thofe who went upon this bufinefs in the barge. We were no fooner clear of the long-boat, than all thofe in the boat with me declared they had the fame intention. When we arrived at the ifland, we were extremely welcome to captain Cheap. The next day, I afked him leave to try if I could prevail upon thofe in the long boat to give us our fhare of provifion : this he granted ; but faid if we went in the barge, they would certainly take her from us. I told him my defign was to walk it, and only defired the boat might land me upon the main, and wait for me

till

till I came back. I had the moft dreadful journey of it imaginable, through thick woods and fwamps all the way; but I might as well have fpared myfelf that trouble, as it was to no manner of pur- pofe; for they would not give me, nor any one of us that left them, a fingle ounce of provifions of any kind. I there- fore returned, and after that made a fe- cond attempt; but all in vain. They even threatened, if we did not return with the barge, they would fetch her by force. It is impoffible to con- ceive the diftreffed fituation we were now in, at the time of the long-boat's departure. I don't mention this event as the occafion of it; by which, if we who were left on the ifland experienced any alteration at all, it was for the better; and which, in all probability, had it been deferred, might have been fatal to the greateft part of us; but at this time, the fubfiftence on which we had hitherto de- pended

pended chiefly, which was the fhell-fifh, were every where, along fhore, eat up; and as to ftock faved from the wreck, it may be guefled what the amount of that might be, when the fhare allotted to the captain, lieutenant Hamilton, and the fur- geon, was no more than fix pieces of beef, as many of pork, and ninety pounds of flour. As to myfelf, and thofe that left the long-boat, it was the leaft revenge they thought they could take of us to with-hold our provifion from us, though at the fame time it was hard and un- juft. For a day or two after our return, there was fome little pittance dealt out to us, yet it was upon the foot of favour; and we were foon left to our ufual in- duftry for a farther fupply. This was now exerted to very little purpofe, for the reafon before affigned; to which may be added, the wreck was now blown up, all her upper works gone, and no hopes of any valuable driftage from her

for

for the future. A weed called flaugh, fried in the tallow of fome candles we had faved, and wild fellery, were our only fare; by which our ftrength was fo much impaired, that we could fcarcely crawl. It was my misfortune too, to labour under a fevere flux, by which I was reduced to a very feeble ftate; fo that in attempting to traverfe the rocks in fearch of fhell-fifh, I fell from one into very deep water, and with difficulty faved my life by fwimming. As the captain was now freed, by the departure of the long boat, from the riotous applications, menaces, and difturbance of an unruly crew, and left at liberty to follow the plan he had refolved upon, of going northward, he began to think ferioufly of putting it in execution; in order to which, a meffage was fent to the deferters, who had feated themfelves on the other fide of the neighbouring Lagoon, to found them, whether they

were

were inclined to join the captain in his undertaking; and if they were, to bring them over to him. For this fett, the party gone off in the long-boat had left an half allowance proportion of the common ſtock of proviſion. Theſe men, upon the propoſal, readily agreed to join their commander; and being conducted to him, increaſed our number to twenty. The boats which remained in our poſ-ſeſſion to carry off all theſe people, were only the barge and yawl, two very crazy bottoms; the broadſide of the laſt was entirely out, and the firſt had ſuffer-ed much in variety of bad weather ſhe had gone through, and was much out of repair. And now our carpenter was gone from us, we had no re-medy for theſe misfortunes, but the little ſkill we had gained from him. However, we made tolerable ſhift to patch up the boats for our purpoſe. In the height of our diſtreſſes, when hunger,

F   which

which feems to include and abforb all others, was moft prevailing, we were cheared with the appearance, once more, of our friendly Indians, as we thought, from whom we hoped for fome relief; but as the confideration was wanting, for which alone they would part with their commodities, we were not at all benefited by their ftay, which was very fhort. The little referve too of flour made by the captain for our fea-ftock when we fhould leave the ifland, was now diminifhed by theft: the thieves, who were three of our men, were however foon difcovered, and two of them apprehended; but the third made his efcape to the woods. Confidering the preffing ftate of our neceffities, this theft was looked upon as a moft heinous crime, and therefore required an extraordinary punifhment: accordingly the captain ordered thefe delinquents to be feverely whipped, and then to be banifhed to an ifland at fome diftance

from

from us ; but before this latter part of
the sentence could be put in execution,
one of them fled ; but the other was put
alone upon a barren island, which afforded not the least shelter ; however, we,
in compassion, and contrary to order,
patched him up a bit of a hut, and
kindled him a fire, and then left the poor
wretch to shift for himself. In two or
three days after, going to the island in our
boat with some little refreshment, such as
our miserable circumstances would admit
of, and with an intent of bringing him
back, we found him dead and stiff. I was
now reduced to the lowest condition by my
illness, which was increased by the vile
stuff I eat, when we were favoured by a
fair day, a thing very extraordinary in
this climate. We instantly took the advantage of it, and once more visited the
last remains of the wreck, her bottom.
Here our pains were repaid with the
great good fortune of hooking up three

F 2   casks

cafks of beef, which were brought fafe to
fhore. This providential fupply could
not have happened at a more feafonable
time than now, when we were afflicted
with the greateft dearth we had ever experienced, and the little ftrength we had
remaining was to be exerted in our endeavours to leave the ifland. Accordingly we foon found a remedy for our
ficknefs, which was nothing but the effects of famine, and were greatly reftored
by food. The provifion was equally
diftributed among us all, and ferved us
for the remainder of our ftay here.

We began to grow extremely impatient to leave the ifland, as the days were
now nearly at their longeft, and about
midfummer in thefe parts ; but as to the
weather, there feems to be little difference
in a difference of feafons. Accordingly,
on the 15th of December, the day being
tolerable, we told captain Cheap we
thought it a fine opportunity to run
acrofs

acrofs the bay. But he firft defired two
or three of us to accompany him to our
place of obfervation, the top of Mount
Mifery; when looking through his per-
fpective, he obferved to us that the fea
ran very high without. However, this
had no weight with the people, who
were defirous, at all events, to be gone.
I fhould here obferve, that captain
Cheap's plan was, if poffible, to get to
the ifland of Chiloe; and if we found
any veffel there, to board her immediately, and cut her out. This he might
certainly have done with eafe, had it
been his good fortune to get round with
the boats. We now launched both boats,
and got every thing on board of them as
quick as poffible. Captain Cheap, the
furgeon, and myfelf, were in the barge
with nine men; and lieutenant Hamilton and Mr. Campbell in the yawl with
fix. I fteered the barge, and Mr. Campbell the yawl; but we had not been two

F 3 hours

hours at fea before the wind fhifted more to the weftward, and began to blow very hard, and the feà ran extremely high; fo that we could no longer keep our heads towards the cape or headland we had defigned for. This cape we had had a view of in one of the intervals of fair weather, during our abode on the ifland, from Mount Mifery; and it feemed to be diftant between twenty and thirty leagues from us. We were now obliged to bear away right before the wind. Though the yawl was not far from us, we could fee nothing of her, except now and then, upon the top of a mountainous fea. In both the boats, the men were obliged to frt as clofe as poffible, to receive the feas on their backs, to prevent their filling us, which was what we every moment expected. We were obliged to throw every thing overboard to lighten the boats, all our beef, and even the grapnel, to prevent finking.

Night

Night was coming on, and we were running on a lee-fhore faft, where the fea broke in a frightful manner. Not one amongft us imagined it poffible for boats to live in fuch a fea. In this fitu-ation, as we neared the fhore, expecting to be beat to pieces by the firft breaker, we perceived a fmall opening between the rocks, which we ftood for, and found a very narrow paffage between them, which brought us into a harbour for the boats as calm and fmooth as a mill-pond. The yawl had got in before us, and our joy was great at meeting again after fo unexpected a deliverance. Here we fecured the boats, and afcended a rock. It rained exceffively hard all the firft part of the night, and was extremely cold ; and though we had not a dry thread about us, and no wood could be found for firing, we were obliged to pafs the night in that uncomfortable fitu-ation, without any covering, fhivering

in

in our wet cloaths. The froft coming on with the morning, it was impoffible for any of us to get a moment's fleep ; and having flung overboard our provifion the day before, there being no profpect of finding any thing to eat on this coaft, in the morning we pulled out of the cove ; but found fo great a fea without, that we could make but little of it. After tugging all day, towards night we put in among fome fmall iflands, landed upon one of them, and found it a mere fwamp. As the weather was the fame, we paffed this night much as we had done the preceding ; fea-tangle was all we could get to eat at firft, but the next day we had better luck ; the furgeon fhot a goofe, and we found materials for a good fire. We were confined here three or four days, the weather all that time proving fo bad that we could not put out. As foon as it grew moderate, we left this place, and fhaped

our

our courfe to the northward; and perceiving a large opening between very
high land and a low point, we fteered
for it; and when got that length, found
a large bay, down which we rowed, flattering ourfelves there might be a paffage
that way; but towards night we came to
the bottom of the bay, and finding no
outlet, we were obliged to return the
fame way we came, having met with nothing the whole day to alleviate our
hunger.

Next night we put into a little cove,
which, from the great quantity of redwood found there, we called Redwood
Cove. Leaving this place in the morning, we had the wind foutherly, blowing
frefh, by which we made much way
that day, to the northward. Towards
evening we were in with a pretty large
ifland. Putting afhore on it, we found
it cloathed with the fineft trees we had
ever feen, their ftems running up to a

prodi-

prodigious height, without knot or
branch, and as ftrait as cedars: the leaf
of thefe trees refembled the myrtle leaf,
only fomewhat larger. I have feen trees
larger than thefe in circumference, on
the coaft of Guinea, and there only ; but
for a length of ftem, which gradually
tapering, I have no where met with any
to compare to them. The wood was of
a hard fubftance, and if not too heavy,
would have made good mafts; the dimenfions of fome of thefe trees being equal
to a main-maft of a firft rate man of
war. The fhore was covered with drift
wood of a very large fize ; moft of it
cedar, which makes a brifk fire ; but is
fo fubject to fnap and fly, that when we
waked in the morning, after a found
fleep, we found our cloaths finged in
many places with the fparks, and covered with fplinters.

The next morning being calm, we
rowed out; but as foon as clear of the
island,

ifland, we found a great fwell from the
weftward; we rowed to the bottom of
a very large bay, which was to the
northward of us, the land very low, and
we were in hopes of finding fome inlet
through, but did not; fo kept along
fhore to the weftward. This part, which
I take to be above fifty leagues from
Wager Ifland, is the very bottom of the
large bay it lays in. Here was the only
paffage to be found, which (if we could
by any means have got information of
it) would have faved us much fruitlefs
labour. Of this paffage I fhall have occafion to fay more hereafter.

Having at this time an off-fhore wind,
we kept the land clofe on board, till we
came to a head land: it was near night
before we got a-breaft of the head-land,
and opening it difcovered a very large
bay to the northward, and another head-
land to the weftward, at a great diftance.
We endeavoured to cut fhort our paffage

to

to it by croffing, which is very feldom
to be effected, in thefe over-grown feas,
by boats: and this we experienced now;
for the wind fpringing up, and beginning to blow frefh, we were obliged to
put back towards the firft head-land,
into a fmall cove, juft big enough to
fhelter the two boats. Here an accident
happened that alarmed us much. After
fecuring our boats we climbed up a rock
fcarcely large enough to contain our
numbers: having nothing to eat, we
betook ourfelves to our ufual receipt for
hunger, which was going to fleep. We
accordingly made a fire, and ftowed ourfelves round it as well as we could; but
two of our men being incommoded for
want of room, went a little way from us,
into a fmall nook, over which a great
cliff hung, and ferved them for a canopy.
In the middle of the night we were awakened with a terrible rumbling, which
we apprehended to be nothing lefs than
the

the shock of an earthquake, which we had before experienced in these parts; and this conjecture we had reason to think not ill founded, upon hearing hollow groans and cries as of men half swallowed up. We immediately got up, and ran to the place from whence the cries came, and then we were put out of all doubt as to the opinion we had formed of this accident; for here we found the two men almost buried under loose stones and earth : but upon a little farther enquiry, we were undeceived as to the cause we had imputed this noise to, which we found to be occasioned by the sudden giving way of the impending cliff, which fell a little beyond our people, carrying trees and rocks with it, and loose earth; the latter of which fell in part on our men, whom we with some pains rescued from their uneasy situation, from which they escaped with some bruises. The next morning we got out early,

early, and the wind being wefterly, rowed the whole day for the head-land we had feen the night before ; but when we had got that length could find no harbour, but were obliged to go into a fandy bay, and lay the whole night upon our oars ; and a moft dreadful one it proved, blowing and raining very hard. Here we were fo pinched with hunger, that we eat the fhoes off our feet, which confifted of raw feal fkin. In the morning we got out of the bay; but the inceffant foul weather had overcome us, and we began to be indifferent as to what befel us ; and the boats, in the night, making into a bay, we nearly loft the yawl, a breaker having filled her, and driven her afhore upon the beach. This, by fome of our accounts, was Chriftmas-day ; but our accounts had fo often been interrupted by our diftreffes, that there was no depending upon them. Upon feeing the yawl in this imminent

6   danger,

danger, the barge ſtood off, and went into another bay to the northward of it, where it was ſmoother lying ; but there was no poſſibility of getting on ſhore. In the night the yawl joined us again. The next day was ſo bad, that we deſpaired reaching the head-land, ſo rowed down the bay in hopes of getting ſome ſeal, as that animal had been ſeen the day before, but met with no ſuccefs ; ſo returned to the ſame bay we had been in the night before, where the ſurf having abated ſomewhat, we went aſhore, and picked up a few ſhell-fiſh. In the morning, we got on board early, and ran along ſhore to the weſtward, for about three leagues, in order to get round a cape, which was the weſternmoſt land we could ſee. It blew very hard, and there ran ſuch a ſea, that we heartily wiſhed ourſelves back again, and accordingly made the beſt of our way for

that

that bay which we had left in the morning ; but before we could reach it night came on, and we paffed a moſt difmal one, lying upon our oars.

The weather continuing very bad, we put in for the ſhore in the morning, where we found nothing but tangle and fea-weed. We now paffed ſome days roving about for proviſions, as the weather was too bad to make another attempt to get round the cape as yet. We found ſome fine Lagoons towards the head of the bay ; and in them killed ſome feal, and got a good quantity of ſhell-fiſh, which was a great relief to us. We now made a ſecond attempt to double the cape; but when we got the length of it, and paffed the firſt headland, for it conſiſts of three of an equal height, we got into a fea that was horrid ; for it ran all in heaps, like the Race of Portland, but much worſe. We

were

were happy to put back again to the old place, with little hopes of ever getting round this cape.

Next day, the weather proving very bad, all hands went aſhore to procure ſome ſuſtenance, except two in each boat, which were left as boat-keepers: this office we took by turns ; and it was now my lot to be upon this duty with another man. The yawl lay within us at a grapnel ; in the night it blew very hard, and a great ſea tumbled in upon the ſhore ; but being extremely fatigued, we in the boats went to ſleep : notwith-ſtanding, however, I was at laſt awakened by the uncommon motion of the boat, and the roaring of the breakers every where about us. At the ſame time I heard a ſhrieking, like to that of perſons in diſtreſs ; I looked out, and ſaw the yawl canted bottom upwards by a ſea, and ſoon afterwards diſappeared. One of our

G   men,

men, whofe name was William Rofe, a
quarter mafter, was drowned; the other
was thrown afhore by the furf, with his
head buried in the fand; but by the immediate affiftance of the people on fhore, was
faved. As for us in the barge, we expected the fame fate every moment; for the fea
broke a long way without us. However, we got her head to it, and hove up
our grapnel, or fhould rather fay kellick,
which we had made to ferve in the
room of our grapnel, hove overboard
fome time before, to lighten the boat.
By this means we ufed our utmoft efforts to pull her without the breakers
fome way, and then let go our kellick
again. Here we lay all the next day,
in a great fea, not knowing what would
be our fate. To add to our mortification, we could fee our companions in tolerable plight afhore, eating feal, while
we were ftarving with hunger and cold.

For

For this month paſt, we had not known
what it was to have a dry thread about
us.

The next day being ſomething more
moderate, we ventured in with the barge
as near as we could to the ſhore, and our
companions threw us ſome ſeals liver;
which having eat greedily, we were
ſeized with exceſſive ſickneſs, which affected us ſo much, that our ſkin peeled
off from head to foot.

Whilſt the people were on ſhore here,
Mr. Hamilton met with a large ſeal, or
ſea-lion, and fired a brace of balls into
him, upon which the animal turned
upon him open-mouthed; but preſently
fixing his bayonet, he thruſt it down
its throat, with a good part of the barrel
of the gun, which the creature bit in
two ſeemingly with as much eaſe as if
it had been a twig. Notwithſtanding
the wounds it received, it eluded all farther efforts to kill it, and got clear off.

I call

I call this animal a large feal, or fea-lion, becaufe it refembles a feal in many particulars ; but then it exceeds it fo much in fize, as to be fufficiently determined, by that diftinction only, to be of another fpecies. Mr. Walter, in Lord Anfon's Voyage, has given a particular defcription of thofe which are feen about Juan Fernandes ; but they have in other climates, different appearances as well as different qualities, as we had occafion to obferve in this, and a late voyage I made. However, as fo much already has been faid of the fea-lion, I fhall only mention two peculiarities ; one relative to its appearance, and the other to its properties of action, which diftinguifh it from thofe defcribed by him. Thofe I faw, were without that fnout, or trunk, hanging below the end of the upper jaw; but then the males were furnifhed with a large fhaggy mane, which gave them a moft formidable appearance. And, whereas,

whereas, he fays, thofe he faw were un-wieldy, and eafily deftroyed, we found fome, on the contrary, that lay at a mile's diftance from the water, which came down upon us, when difturbed, with fuch impetuofity, that it was as much as we could do to get out of their way ; and when attacked, would turn upon us with great agility.

Having loft the yawl, and being too many for the barge to carry off, we were compelled to leave four of our men be-hind. They were all marines, who feem-ed to have no great objection to the de-termination made with regard to them, fo exceedingly difheartened and worn out were they with the diftreffes and dan-gers they had already gone through. And, indeed, I believe it would have been a matter of indifference to the greateft part of the reft, whether they fhould em-bark, or take their chance. The captain diftributed to thefe poor fellows arms

and

and ammunition, and fome other necef-
faries. When we parted, they ftood upon the beach, giving us three cheers,
and called out, God blefs the king.
We faw them a little after, fetting
out upon their forlorn hope, and help-
ing one another over a hideous tract
of rocks; but confidering the difficulties attending this only way of tra-
velling left them; for the woods are
impracticable, from their thicknefs,
and the deep fwamp every where to be
met in them; confidering too, that
the coaft here is rendered fo inhofpitable, by the heavy feas that are conftantly tumbling upon it, as not to
afford even a little fhell-fifh, it is
probable that all met with a miferable
end.

We rowed along fhore to the weftward, in order to make one more attempt to double the cape: when abreaft
of the firft head-land there ran fuch a fea,

8   that

that we expected, every inftant, the boat
would go down. But as the prefervation of life had now, in a great meafure,
loft its actuating principle upon us, we
ftill kept pufhing through it, till we
opened a bay to the northward. In all
my life, I never faw fo dreadful a fea as
drove in here; it began to break at more
than half a mile from the fhore. Perceiving now that it was impoffible for
any boat to get round, the men lay upon
their oars till the boat was very near the
breakers, the mountainous fwell that
then ran, heaving her in at a great rate.
I thought it was their intention to put
an end to their lives and mifery at once;
but nobody fpoke for fome time. At
laft, captain Cheap told them, they muft
either perifh immediately, or pull ftoutly
for it to get off the fhore; but they might
do as they pleafed. They chofe, however, to exert themfelves a little, and
after infinite difficulty, got round the

G 4 head-

head-land again, giving up all thoughts of making any further attempt to double the cape. It was night before we could get back to the bay, where we were compelled to leave four of our men, in order to fave, if poffible, the remainder; for we muft all have certainly perifhed, if more than fixteen had been crouded into fo fmall a boat: This bay we named Marine Bay. When we had returned to this bay, we found the furf ran fo high, that we were obliged to lay upon our oars all night; and it was now refolved to go back to Wager's Ifland, there to linger out a miferable life, as we had not the leaft profpect of returning home.

But before we fet out, in confequence of this refolution, it was neceffary, if poffible, to get fome little ftock of feal to fupport us in a paffage, upon which, wherever we might put in, we were not likely to meet with any fupply. Accordingly,

cordingly, it was determined to go up
that Lagoon in which we had before got
fome feal, to provide ourfelves with fome
more ; but we did not leave the bay till
we had made fome fearch after the unhappy marines we had left on fhore.
Could we have found them, we had now
agreed to take them on board again,
though it would have been the certain
deftruction of us all. This, at another
time, would have been mere madnefs ;
but we were now refigned to our fate,
which we none of us thought far off ;
however, there was nothing to be feen
of them, and no traces but a mufket on
the beach.

Upon returning up the Lagoon, we
were fo fortunate as to kill fome feal,
which we boiled, and laid in the boat
for fea-ftock. While we were ranging
along fhore in detached parties, in queft
of this, and whatever other eatable
might come in our way, our furgeon,

who

who was then by himfelf, difcovered a
pretty large hole, which feemed to lead
to fome den, or repofitory, within the
rocks. It was not fo rude, or natural, but that there were fome figns of its
having been cleared, and made more acceffible by induftry. The furgeon for
fome time hefitated whether he fhould
venture in, from his uncertainty as to the
reception he might meet with from any
inhabitant ; but his curiofity getting the
better of his fears, he determined to go
in ; which he did upon his hands and
knees, as the paffage was too low for
him to enter otherwife. After having
proceeded a confiderable way thus, he
arrived at a fpacious chamber ; but whether hollowed out by hands, or natural,
he could not be pofitive. The light into
this chamber was conveyed through a
hole at the top; in the midft was a kind
of bier, made of fticks laid croffways,
fupported by props of about five foot in
height.

height. Upon this bier, five or fix bodies were extended ; which, in appearance, had been depofited there a long
time; but had fuffered no decay or diminution. They were without covering,
and the flefh of thefe bodies was become
perfectly dry and hard ; which, whether
done by any art, or fecret, the favages
may be poffeffed of, or occafioned by
any drying virtue in the air of the cave,
could not be gueffed. Indeed, the furgeon, finding nothing there to eat,
which was the chief inducement for his
creeping into this hole, did not amufe
himfelf with long difquifitions, or make
that accurate examination which he
would have done at another time ; but
crawling out as he came in, he went
and told the firft he met of what he had
feen. Some had the curiofity to go in
likewife. I had forgot to mention that
there was another range of bodies, depofited in the fame manner, upon another

platform

platform under the bier. Probably this
was the burial place of their great men,
called caciques; but from whence they
could be brought, we were utterly at a lofs
to conceive, there being no traces of any
Indian fettlement hereabout. We had
feen no favage fince we left the ifland,
or obferved any marks in the coves, or
bays to the northward, where we had
touched, fuch as of fire-places, or old
wigwams, which they never fail of leaving behind them ; and it is very probable,
from the violent feas that are always
beating upon this coaft, its deformed af-
pect, and the very fwampy foil that
every where borders upon it, that it is
little frequented.

We now croffed the firft bay for the
head-land we left on Chriftmas day,
much dejected; for under our former
fufferings, we were in fome meafure
fupported with the hopes that, as we advanced, however little, they were fo much
the

the nearer their termination; but now
our profpect was difmal and difpiriting,
indeed, as we had the fame difficulties
and dangers to encounter, not only without any flattering views to leffen them,
but under the aggravating circumftance
of their leading to an inevitable and
miferable death; for we could not poffibly conceive that the fate of ftarving
could be avoided by any human means,
upon that defolate ifland we were returning to. The fhell-fifh, which was the only
fubfiftence that ifland had hitherto afforded in any meafure, was exhaufted;
and the Indians had fhewn themfelves fo
little affected by the common incitements
of compaffion, that we had no hopes to
build upon any impreffions of that fort
in them. They had already refufed to
barter their dogs with us, for want of a
valuable commodity on our fide; fo that
it is wonderful we did not give ourfelves up to defpondency, and lay afide

all

all farther attempts; but we were fupported by that invifible Power, who can
make the moſt untoward circumſtances
fubſervient to his gracious purpoſes.

At this time, our uſual bad weather
attended us; the night too fet in long
before we could reach the cove we before
had taken fhelter in; fo that we were
obliged to keep the boat's head to the
fea all night, the fea every where a-ſtern
of us, running over hideous breakers.
In the morning, we defigned ſtanding
over for that iſland in which we had obferved thoſe ſtrait and lofty trees before-
mentioned, and which captain Cheap
named Montroſe Iſland; but as foon as
we opened the head-land to the weſtward of us, a fudden fquall took the
boat, and very near overſet her. We were
inſtantly full of water; but by baling
with our hats and hands, and any thing
that would hold water, we with difficulty freed her. Under this alarming

circum-

circumftance, we found it advifeable to
return back and put into the cove,
which the night before we were prevented getting into. We were detained
here two or three days, by exceeding
bad weather; fo that, had we not fortunately provided ourfelves with fome
feal, we muft have ftarved, for this place
afforded us nothing.

At length we reached Montrofe Ifland.
This is by much the beft and pleafanteft
fpot we had feen in this part of the world;
though it has nothing on it eatable but
fome berries, which refembled goofeberries in flavour: they are of a black
hue, and grow in fwampy ground; and
the bufh, or tree, that bears them is much
taller than that of our goofeberries.
We remained here fome time, living
upon thefe berries, and the remainder
of our feal, which was now grown quite
rotten. Our two or three firft attempts
to put out from this ifland were with-

out

out fuccefs, the tempeftuous weather obliging us fo often to put back again. One of our people was much inclined to remain here, thinking it at leaft as good a place as Wager's Ifland to end his days upon ; but he was obliged by the reft to go off with them. We had not been long out before it began to blow a ftorm of wind ; and the mift came on fo thick, that we could not fee the land, and were at a lofs which way to fteer; but we heard the fea, which ran exceedingly high, breaking near us ; upon which we immediately hauled aft the fheet, and hardly weathered the breakers by a boat's length. At the fame time we fhipped a fea that nearly filled us : it ftruck us with that violence as to throw me, and one or two more, down into the bottom of the boat, where we were half drowned before we could get up again. This was .one of the moft extraordinary efcapes we had in

the

the courfe of this expedition ; for captain Cheap, and every one elfe, had
entirely given themfelves up for loft.
However, it pleafed God that we got
that evening into Redwood Cove, where
the weather continued fo bad all night,
we could keep no fire in to dry ourfelves
with ; but there being no other alterna-
tive for us, but to ftay here and ftarve,
or put to fea again, we chofe the latter,
and put out in the morning again,
though the weather was very little
mended. In three or four days after,
we arrived at our old ftation, Wager's
ifland; but in fuch a miferable plight, that
though we thought our condition upon fetting out would not admit of any additional
circumftance of mifery, yet it was to be
envied in comparifon of what we now
fuffered, fo worn and reduced were we
by fatigue and hunger ; having eat nothing for fome days but fea-weed and
tangle. Upon this expedition, we had

H   been

been out, by our account, juft two months ; in which we had rounded, backwards and forwards, the great bay formed to the northward by that high land we had obferved from Mount Mi-fery.

The firft thing we did upon our arrival, was to fecure the barge, as this was our fole dependence for any relief that might offer by fea ; which done, we repaired to our huts, which formed a kind of village or ftreet, confifting of feveral irregular habitations ; fome of which being covered by a kind of brufh-wood thatch, afforded tolerable fhelter againft the inclemency of the weather. Among thefe, there was one which we obferved with fome furprife to be nailed up. We broke it open, and found fome iron work, picked out with much pains from thofe pieces of the wreck which were driven afhore. We concluded from hence, that the Indians

who

who had been here in our abfence, were
not of that tribe with which we had
fome commerce before, who feemed to
fet no value upon iron, but from fome
other quarter ; and muft have had communication with the Spaniards, from
whom they had learned the value and
ufe of that commodity. Thieving from
ftrangers is a commendable talent among
favages in general, and befpeaks an addrefs which they much admire ; though
the ftricteft honefty, with regard to the
property of each other, is obferved
among them. There is no doubt but they
ranfacked all our houfes ; but the men
had taken care, before they went off in
the long-boat, to ftrip them of their moft
valuable furniture ; that is, the bales
of cloth ufed for lining, and converted them into trowfers and watch-
coats. Upon farther fearch, we found,
thrown afide in the bufhes, at the back
of one of the huts, fome pieces of feal,
in a very putrid condition ; which, how-

ever.

ever, our ftomachs were far from loath-
ing. The next bufinefs which the people fet about very ferioufly, was to proceed to Mount Mifery, and bury the
corpfe of the murdered perfon, mentioned
to have been difcovered there fome little
time after our being caft away; for to
the neglect of this neceffary tribute to
that unfortunate perfon, the men affigned all their ill fuccefs upon the late
expedition.

That common people in general are
addicted to fuperftitious conceits, is an
obfervation founded on experience; and
the reafon is evident: but I cannot allow that common feamen are more fo
than others of the lower clafs. In the
moft enlightened ages of antiquity, we
find it to have been the popular opinion,
that the fpirits of the dead were not at
reft till their bodies were interred; and
that they did not ceafe to haunt and
trouble thofe who had neglected this
duty

duty to the departed. This is still believed by the vulgar, in most countries;
and in our men, this persuasion was
much heightened by the melancholy condition they were reduced to; and
was farther confirmed by an occurrence
which happened some little time before
we went upon our last expedition. One
night we were alarmed with a strange cry,
which resembled that of a man drowning. Many of us ran out of our huts
towards the place from whence the noise
proceeded, which was not far off shore;
where we could perceive, but not diftinctly (for it was then moon light), an
appearance like that of a man swim-
ming half out of water. The noise
that this creature uttered was so unlike
that of any animal they had heard before, that it made a great impression upon the men; and they frequently re-
called this apparition at the time of their
distresses, with reflexions on the neglect

H 3   of

of the office they were now fulfilling.

We were foon driven again to the
greateft ftraits for want of fomething to
fubfift upon, by the extreme bad weather
that now fet in upon us. Wild fellery
was all we could procure, which raked
our ftomachs inftead of affuaging our
hunger. That dreadful and laft refource
of men, in not much worfe circumftances than ours, of configning one man
to death for the fupport of the reft, began to be mentioned in whifpers; and
indeed there were fome among us who,
by eating what they found raw, were become little better than canibals. But
fortunately for us, and opportunely to
prevent this horrid proceeding, Mr. Hamilton, at this time, found fome rotten
pieces of beef, caft up by the fea at fome
miles diftance from the huts, which he,
though a temptation which few would
have refifted in parallel circumftances,
fcorned

fcorned to conceal from the reft ; but generoufly diftributed among us.

A few days after, the myftery of the nailing up of the hut, and what had been doing by the Indians upon the ifland in our abfence, was partly explained to us ; for about the 15th day after our return, there came a party of Indians to the ifland in two canoes, who were not a little furprifed to find us here again. Among thefe, was an Indian of the tribe of the Chonos, who live in the neighbourhood of Chiloe *. He talked the Spanifh language ; but with that favage accent which renders it almoft unintelligible to any but thofe who are adepts in that language. He was likewife a cacique, or leading man of his tribe; which authority was confirmed to him by the Spaniards ; for he carried the ufual badge

---

* Chiloe is an ifland on the weftern coaft of America, about the 43d deg. of S. latitude ; and the fout-hernmoft fettlement under the Spanifh jurifdiction on that coaft.

and

and mark of diftinction by which the Spaniards, and their dependents, hold their military and civil employments; which is a ftick with a filver head. Thefe badges, of which the Indians are very vain, at once ferve to retain the cacique in the ftrongeft attachment to the Spanifh government, and give him greater weight with his own dependents : yet, withal, he is the mereft flave, and has not one thing he can call his own. This report of our fhipwreck (as we fuppofed) having reached the Chonos, by means of the intermediate tribes, which handed it to one another, from thofe Indians who firft vifited us ; this cacique was either fent to learn the truth of the rumour, or having firft got the intelligence, fet out with a view of making fome advantage of the wreck, and appropriating fuch iron-work as he could gather from it to his own ufe : for that metal is become very valuable to thofe favages, fince their

commerce

commerce with the Spaniards has taught them to apply it to feveral purpofes. But as the fecreting any thing from a rapacious Spanifh rey, or governor (even an old rufty nail), by any of their Indian dependents, is a very dangerous offence, he was careful to conceal the little prize he had made, till he could conveniently carry it away ; for in order to make friends of thefe favages, we had left their hoard untouched.

Our furgeon, Mr. Elliot, being mafter of a few Spanifh words, made himfelf fo far underftood by the cacique as to let him know, that our intention was to reach fome of the Spanifh fettlements, if we could ; that we were unacquainted with the beft and fafeft way, and what track was moft likely to afford us fubfiftence in our journey ; promifing, if he would undertake to conduct us in the barge, he fhould have it, and every thing in it, for his trouble, as foon as it had

ferved

ferved our prefent occafions. To thefe
conditions the cacique, after much perfuafion, at length, agreed. Accordingly, having made the beft preparation we could,
we embarked on board the barge to the
number of fifteen, including the cacique,
whofe name was Martin, and his fervant Emanuel. We were, indeed, fixteen, when we returned from our laft
fruitlefs attempt to get off the ifland;
but we had buried two fince that, who
perifhed with hunger; and a marine,
having committed theft, run away to
avoid the punifhment his crime deferved,
and hid himfelf in the woods; fince
which he was never heard of. We
now put off, accompanied with the two
Indian canoes; in one of which was a
favage, with his two wives, who had an
air of dignity fuperior to the reft, and
was handfome in his perfon. He had
his hut, during his ftay with us, feparate
from the other Indians, who feemed to

pay

pay him extraordinary refpect; but in two
or three nights, thefe Indians, being inde-
pendent of the Spaniards, and living
fomewhere to the fouthward of our
Chono guide, left us to proceed on our
journey by ourfelves.

The firft night we lay at an ifland def-
titute of all refrefhment; where having
found fome fhelter for our boat, and
made ourfelves a fire, we flept by it.
The next night we were more unfortunate, though our wants were increafing;
for having run to the weftward of Mon-
trofs ifland, we found no fhelter for the
barge; but were under the neceffity of
lying upon our oars, fuffering the moft
extreme pangs of hunger. The next day
brought us to the bottom of a great bay,
where the Indian guide had left his
family, a wife and two children, in a
hut. Here we ftaid two or three days,
during which we were conftantly employed

ployed in ranging along fhore in queft
of fhell-fifh.

We now again proceeded on our voyage, having received on board the family
of our guide, who conducted us to a river, the ftream of which was fo rapid,
that after our utmoft efforts from morning to evening, we gained little upon the
current; and at laft were obliged to defift from our attempt, and return. I had
hitherto fteered the boat; but one of our
men finking under the fatigue, expired
foon after, which obliged me to take the
oar in his room, and row againft this
heart-breaking ftream. Whilft I was thus
employed, one of our men whofe name
was John Bofman, though hitherto the
ftouteft man among us, fell from his
feat under the thwarts, complaining that
his ftrength was quite exhaufted for want
of food, and that he fhould die very
fhortly. As he lay in this condition, he
would

would every now and then break out in the moft pathetic wifhes for fome little fuftenance ; that two or three mouthfuls might be the means of faving his life. The captain, at this time, had a large piece of boiled feal by him, and was the only one that was provided with any thing like a meal ; but we were become fo hardened againft the impreffions of others fufferings by our own ; fo familiarized to fcenes of this, and every other kind of mifery ; that the poor man's dying entreaties were vain. I fat next to him when he dropped, and having a few dried fhell-fifh (about five or fix) in my pocket, from time to time put one in his mouth, which ferved only to prolong his pains ; from which, however, foon after my little fupply failed, he was releafed by death. For this, and another man I mentioned a little before to have expired under the like circumftances, when we returned

returned from this unfuccefsful enter-
prize, we made a grave in the fands.

It would have redounded greatly to
the tendernefs and humanity of captain
Cheap, if at this time he had remitted
fomewhat of that attention he fhewed to
felf-prefervation ; which is hardly allow-
able but where the confequence of relieving others muft be immediately and
manifeftly fatal to ourfelves ; but I
would venture to affirm, that in thefe
laft affecting exigencies, as well as fome
others, a fparing perhaps adequate to the
emergency, might have been admitted
confiftently with a due regard to his own
neceffities. The captain had better opportunities of recruiting his ftock than
any of us ; for his rank was confidered
by the Indian as a reafon for fupplying
him when he would not find a bit for us.
Upon the evening of the day in which
thefe difafters happened, the captain producing

ducing a large piece of boiled feal, fuffered no one to partake with him but
the furgeon, who was the only man in
favour at this time. We did not expect,
indeed, any relief from him in our prefent condition ; for we had a few fmall
mufcles and herbs to eat ; but the men
could not help expreffing the greateft in-
dignation at his neglect of the deceafed ;
faying that he deferved to be deferted
by the reft for his favage behaviour.

The endeavoring to pafs up this river
was for us, who had fo long ftruggled
with hunger, a moft unfeafonable attempt ; by which we were harraffed to
a degree that threatened to be fatal to
more of us ; but our guide, without any
refpect to the condition our hardfhips
had reduced us to, was very follicitous
for us to go that way, which poffibly he
had gone before in light canoes ; but for
fuch a boat as ours was impracticable.
We conceived, therefore, at that time,

6   that

that this was fome fhort cut, which was
to bring us forward in our voyage; but
we had reafon to think afterwards, that
the greater probability there was of his
getting the barge, which was the wages
of his undertaking, fafe to his fettlement
by this, rather than another courfe, was
his motive for preferring it to the way we
took afterwards, where there was a carrying place of confiderable length, over
which it would have been impoffible to
have carried our boat.

The country hereabouts wears the
moft uncouth, defolate, and rugged af-
pect imaginable; it is fo circumftanced
as to difcourage the moft fanguine adventurers from attempts to fettle it: were
it for no other reafon than the conftant
heavy rains, or rather torrents, which
pour down here, and the vaft fea and furf
which the prevailing wefterly winds im-
pel upon this coaft, it muft be rendered
inhofpitable. All entrance into the
woods

(113)

woods is not only extremely difficult, but
hazardous ; not from any affaults you
are likely to meet with from wild
beafts ; for even thefe could hardly find
convenient harbour here ; but from the
deep fwamp, which is the reigning foil
of this country, and in which the woods
may be faid rather to float than grow;
fo that, except upon a range of deformed
broken rocks which form the fea coaft,
the traveller cannot find found footing
any where. With this unpromifing
fcene before us we were now fetting out
in fearch of food, which nothing but the
moft preffing inftances of hunger could
induce us to do: we had, indeed, the
young Indian fervant to our cacique for
our conductor, who was left by him to
fhew us where the fhell-fifh was moft
plenty. The cacique was gone with the
reft of his family, in the canoe, with a
view of getting fome feal, upon a trip

I   which

which would detain him from us three
or four days.

After fearching the coaft fome time
with very little fuccefs, we began to think
of returning to the barge; but fix of the
men, with the Indian, having advanced
fome few paces before the officers, got
into the boat firft ; which they had no
fooner done than they put off, and left
us, to return no more. And now all the
difficulties we had hitherto endured,
feemed light in comparifon of what we
expected to fuffer from this treachery of
our men, who, with the boat, had taken
away every thing that might be the means
of preferving our lives. The little
cloaths we had faved from the wreck,
our mufkets and ammunition, were gone,
except a little powder, which muft be
preferved for kindling fires, and one
gun, which I had, and was now become
ufelefs for want of ammunition ; and all
thefe wants were now come upon us at

a time

a time when we could not be worfe fitu-
ated for fupplying them. Yet under
thefe difmal and forlorn appearances
was our delivery now preparing; and
from thefe hopelefs circumftances were
we to draw hereafter an inftance fcarce
to be parallelled, of the unfearchable
ways of Providence. It was at that
time little fufpected by us, that the
barge, in which we founded all our
hopes of efcaping from this favage
coaft, would certainly have proved the
fatal caufe of detaining us till we were
confumed by the labour and hardfhips
requifite to row her round the capes and
great head lands; for it was impoffible
to carry her by land, as we did the boats
of the Indians. At prefent, no condition could be worfe than we thought
ours to be: there ran at this time a very
high fea, which breaking with great
fury upon this coaft, made it very impro-
bable that fuftenance in any proportion

to our wants could be found upon it;
yet, unpromifing as this profpect was,
and though little fuccour could be expected from this quarter, I could not
help, as I ftrolled along fhore from the
reft, cafting my eyes towards the fea.
Continuing thus to look out, I thought
I faw fomething now and then upon
the top of a fea that looked black,
which upon obferving ftill more in-
tently, I imagined at laft to be a canoe;
but reflecting afterwards how unufual
it was for Indians to venture out in fo
mountainous a fea, and at fuch a diftance from the land, I concluded myfelf
to be deceived. However, its nearer approach convinced me, beyond all doubt,
of its being a canoe ; but that it could
not put in any where hereabouts, but intended for fome other part of the coaft.
I ran back as faft as I could to my companions, and acquainted them with what
I had feen. The defpondency they were

in

in would not allow them to give credit
to it at firſt; but afterwards, being convinced that it was as I reported it, we
were all in the greateſt hurry to ſtrip off
ſome of our rags to make a ſignal withal,
which we fixed upon a long pole. This
had the deſired effect: the people in the
canoe ſeeing the ſignal, made towards
the land at about two miles diſtance
from us; for no boat could approach
the land where we were: there they put
into a ſmall cove, ſheltered by a large
ledge of rocks without, which broke the
violence of the ſea. Captain Cheap and
I walked along ſhore, and got to the
cove about the time they landed. Here
we found the perſons arrived in this canoe, to be our Indian guide and his wife,
who had left us ſome days before. He
would have aſked us many queſtions;
but neither captain Cheap nor I under-
ſtanding Spaniſh at that time, we took
him along with us to the ſurgeon, whom

I 3　　　　　we

we had left fo ill that he could hardly
raife himfelf from the ground. When the
Indian began to confer with the furgeon,
the firft queftion was, What was become
of the barge and his companion ? and as
he could give him no fatisfactory anfwer to this queftion, the Indian took it
for granted that Emanuel was murdered
by us, and that he and his family ran the
fame rifk ; upon which he was preparing
to provide for his fecurity, by leaving us
directly. The furgeon feeing this, did
all in his power to pacify him, and con-
vince him of the unreafonablenefs of
his apprehenfions ; which he at length
found means to do, by affuring him
that the Indian would come to no harm,
but that he would foon fee him return
fafe; which providentially, and beyond
our expectation, happened accordingly ;
for in a few days after, Emanuel having
contrived to make his efcape from the
people in the barge, returned by ways
that

that were impaffable to any creature but
an Indian. All that we could learn
from Emanuel relative to his efcape was,
that he took the firft opportunity of
leaving them; which was upon their
putting into a bay fomewhere to the
weftward.

We had but one gun among us, and
that was a fmall fowling piece of mine;
no ammunition but a few charges of
powder I had about me; and as the
Indian was very defirous of returning
to the place where he had left his wife
and canoe, Captain Cheap defired I
would go with him and watch over him
all night, to prevent his getting away.
Accordingly I fet out with him; and
when he and his family betook themfelves to reft in the little wigwam they
had made for that purpofe, I kept my
ftation as centinel over them all night.

The next morning captain Cheap, Mr.
Hamilton, and the furgeon, joined us:

the

the latter, by illnefs, being reduced to the moft feeble condition, was fupported by Mr. Hamilton and Mr. Campbel. After holding fome little confultation together, as to the beft manner of proceeding in our journey, it was agreed, that the Indian fhould haul his canoe, with our affiftance, over land, quite acrofs the ifland we were then upon, and put her into a bay on the other fide, from whence he was to go in queft of fome other Indians, by whom he expected to be joined : but as his canoe was too fmall to carry more than three or four perfons, he thought it advifeable to take only captain Cheap and myfelf with him, and to leave his wife and children as pledges with our companions till his return.

As it was matter of uncertainty whether we fhould ever recover the barge or not, which was ftipulated on our fide, to become the property of the cacique,

upon

upon his fulfilling his engagements
with us ; the inducements we now
made ufe of to prevail upon him to proceed with us in our journey were, that
he fhould have my fowling-piece, fome
little matters in the poffeffion of captain
Cheap, and that we would ufe our intereft to procure him fome fmall pecuni-
ary reward.

We were now to fet off in the canoe,
in which I was to affift him in rowing.
Accordingly, putting from this ifland,
we rowed hard all this day and the next,
without any thing to eat but a fcrap of feal,
a very fmall portion of which fell to my
fhare. About two hours after the clofe
of the day, we put afhore, where we
difcovered fix or feven wigwams. For
my part, my ftrength was fo exhaufted
with fatigue and hunger, that it would
have been impoffible for me to have
held out another day at this toilfome
work.

work. As foon as we landed, the Indian
conducted captain Cheap with him into a
wigwam; but I was left to fhift for myfelf.

Thus left, I was for fome time at a lofs
what I had beft do; for knowing that
in the variety of difpofitions obfervable
among the Indians, the furly and favage
temper is the moft prevalent, I had good
reafon to conclude, that if I obtruded
myfelf upon them, my reception would
be but indifferent. Neceffity, however,
put me upon the rifk; I accordingly
pufhed into the next wigwam upon my
hands and knees; for the entrance into
thefe kind of buildings is too low to
admit of any other manner of getting
into them. To give a fhort defcription
of thefe temporary houfes, called wigwams, may not be improper here, for
the fatisfaction of thofe who never faw
any; efpecially as they differ fomewhat
from thofe of North America, which are
more

more generally known from the numerous accounts of that country.

When the Indians of this part of the world have occafion to ftop any where in their rambles, if it be only for a night or two, the men, who take this bufinefs upon them, while the women are employed in much more laborious offices, fuch as diving in the fea for fea-eggs, and fearching the rocks for fhell-fifh, getting fuel, &c. repair to the woods, and cutting a fufficient number of tall, ftrait branches, fix them in an irregular kind of circle, of uncertain dimenfions; which having done, they bend the extremities of thefe branches fo as to meet in a centre at top, where they bind them by a kind of woodbine, called fupple-jack, which they fplit by holding it in their teeth. This frame, or fkeleton of a hut, is made tight againft the weather with a covering of boughs and bark; but as the bark is not got without fome

trouble,

trouble, they generally take it with them when they remove, putting it at the bottom of their canoes : the reft of the wigwam they leave ftanding. The fire is made in the middle of the wigwam, round which they fit upon boughs; and as there is no vent for the fmoke, befides the door-way, which is very low, except through fome crevices, which cannot eafily be flopped, they are not a little incommoded on that account ; and the eyes of fome of them are much affected by it.

But to return: in this wigwam, into which I took the liberty to introduce myfelf, I found only two women, who, upon firft feeing a figure they were not accuftomed to, and fuch a figure too as I then made, were ftruck with aftonifhment. They were fitting by a fire, to which I approached without any apology. However inclined I might have been to make one, my ignorance of their language

language made it impoffible to attempt it. One of thefe women appeared to be young, and very handfome
for an Indian; the other old, and
as frightful as it is poffible to conceive any thing in human fhape to be.
Having ftared at me fome little time,
they both went out; and I, without
farther ceremony, fat me down by the
fire to warm myfelf, and dry the rags I
wore. Yet I cannot fay my fituation
was very eafy, as I expected every inftant to fee two or three men come in
and thruft me out, if they did not deal
with me in a rougher manner.

Soon after the two women came in
again, having, as I fuppofed, conferred
with the Indian, our conductor; and appearing to be in great good humour,
began to chatter and laugh immoderate-
ly. Perceiving the wet and cold condition I was in, they feemed to have compaffion on me, and the old woman went
out

out and brought fome wood, with which fhe made a good fire; but my hunger being impatient, I could not forbear expreffing my defire that they would extend their hofpitality a little further, and bring me fomething to eat. They foon comprehended my meaning, and the younger beginning to rummage under fome pieces of bark that lay in the corner of the wigwam, produced a fine large fifh : this they prefently put upon the fire to broil; and when it was juft warm through, they made a fign for me to eat. They had no need to repeat the invitation; I fell to, and difpatched it in fo fhort a time, that I was in hopes they would comprehend, without further tokens, that I was ready for another; but it was of no confequence, for their ftock of eatables was entirely exhaufted.

After fitting fome time in conference together, in which converfation I could

bear

bear no part, the women made fome figns to me to lay down and go to fleep, firſt having ſtrewed fome dry boughs upon the ground. I laid myſelf down, and foon fell faſt afleep; and about three or four hours after awaking, I found myſelf covered with a bit of blanket, made of the down of birds, which the women uſually wear about their waiſt. The young woman, who had carefully covered me, whilſt fleeping, with her own blanket, was lying clofe by me: the old woman lay on the other fide of her. The fire was low, and almoſt burnt out; but as foon as they found me awake they renewed it, by putting on more fuel. What I had hitherto eat ferved only to fharpen my appetite; I could not help, therefore, being earneſt with them to get me fome more victuals. Having underſtood my neceſſities, they talked together fome little time; after which getting up, they both

went

went out, taking with them a couple of dogs, which they train to affift them in fifhing. After an hour's abfence, they came in trembling with cold, and their hair ftreaming with water, and brought two fifh; which having broiled, they gave me the largeft fhare; and then we all laid down as before to reft.

In the morning, my curiofity led me to vifit the neighbouring wigwams, in which were only one or two men; the reft of the inhabitants were all women and children. I then proceeded to enquire after captain Cheap and our Indian guide, whom I found in the wigwam they at firft occupied : the authority of the cacique had procured the captain no defpicable entertainment. We could not learn what bufinefs the men, whofe wives and children were here left behind, were gone out upon ; but as they feldom or never go upon fifhing-parties (for they have no hunting here) without

7   their

their wives, who take the moſt laborious
part of this purſuit upon themſelves, it
is probable they were gone upon ſome
warlike expedition, in which they uſe
bows and arrows ſometimes, but always
the lance. This weapon they throw
with great dexterity and force, and
never ſtir abroad without it. About
this time their return was looked for ;
a hearing by no means pleaſant to me ;
I was, therefore, determined to enjoy
myſelf as long as they were abſent, and
make the moſt of the good fare I was
poſſeſſed of ; to the pleaſure of which I
thought a little cleanlineſs might in
ſome meaſure contribute ; I therefore
went to a brook, and taking off my ſhirt,
which might be ſaid to be alive with
vermin, ſet myſelf about to waſh it ;
which having done as well as I could,
and hung on a buſh to dry, I heard a
buſtle about the wigwams ; and ſoon
perceived that the women were prepar-

K   ing

ing to depart, having ftripped their wigwams of their bark covering, and carried it into their canoes. Putting on,
therefore, my fhirt juft as it was, I
haftened to join them, having a great
defire of being prefent at one of their
fifhing parties.

It was my lot to be put into the canoe
with my two patroneffes, and fome
others who affifted in rowing : we were
in all four canoes. After rowing fome
time, they gained fuch an offing as they
required, where the water here was about
eight or ten fathom deep, and there lay
upon their oars. And now the youngeft
of the two women, taking a bafket in
her mouth, jumped overboard, and diving to the bottom, continued under water an amazing time : when fhe had filled the bafket with fea-eggs, fhe came
up to the boat-fide; and delivering it fo
filled to the other women in the boat,
they took out the contents, and returned

it

it to her. The diver then, after having taken a fhort time to breathe, went down and up again with the fame fuccefs ; and fo feveral times for the fpace of half an hour. It feems as if Providence had endued this people with a kind of am-phibious nature, as the fea is the only fource from whence almoft all their fub-fiftence is derived. This element too, being here very boifterous, and falling with a moft heavy furf upon a rugged coaft, very little, except fome feal, is to be got any where but in the quiet bo-fom of the deep. What occafions this reflexion is the early propenfity I had fo frequently obferved in the children of thefe favages to this occupation; who, even at the age of three years, might be feen crawling upon their hands and knees among the rocks and breakers ; from which they would tumble them-felves into the fea without regard to the cold, which is here often intenfe ; and

K 2　　　　　fhewing

fhewing no fear of the noife and roaring of the furf.

This fea egg is a fhell-fifh, from
which feveral prickles projeдt in all di-
reдtions, by means whereof it removes
itfelf from place to place. In it are found
four or five yolks, refembling the inner
divifions of an orange, which are of a
very nutritive quality, and excellent
flavour.

The water was at this time extremely
cold ; and when the divers got into the
boats, they feemed greatly benumbed ;
and it is ufual with them after this exercife, if they are near enough their wigwams, to run to the fire ; to which prefenting one fide, they rub and chafe it for
fome time ; then turning the other, ufe it
in the fame manner, till the circula-
tion of the blood is reftored. This
praдtice, if it has no worfe effeдt, muft
occafion their being more fufceptible of
the impreffiohs of cold, than if they
waited

waited the gradual advances of their natural warmth in the open air. I leave it to the decifion of the gentlemen of the faculty, whether this too hafty approach to the fire may not fub-ject them to a diforder I obferved among them, called the elephantiafis, or fwelling of the legs *.

The divers having returned to their boats, we continued to row till towards evening, when we landed upon a low point. As foon as the canoes were hauled up, they employed themfelves in

---

* There are two very different diforders incident to the human body, which bear the fame name, derived from fome refemblance they hold with different parts of the animal fo well known in the countries to which thefe diforders are peculiar. That which was firft fo named is the leprofy, which brings a fcurf on the fkin not unlike the hide of an elephant. The other affects the patient with fuch enormous fwellings of the legs and feet, that they give the idea of thofe fhapelefs pillars which fupport that creature; and therefore this difeafe has alfo been called elephantiafis by the Arabian phyficians; who, together with the Malabarians, among whom it is endemial, attribute it to the drinking bad waters, and the too fudden tranfitions from heat to cold.

K 3   erecting

erecting their wigwams, which they difpatch with great addrefs and quick-nefs. I ftill enjoyed the protection of my two good Indian women, who made me their gueft here as before; they firft regaled me with fea-eggs, and then went out upon another kind of fifhery by the means of dogs and nets. Thefe dogs are a cur-like looking ani-mal; but very fagacious, and eafily trained to this bufinefs. Though in appearance an uncomfortable fort of fport; yet they engage in it readily, feem to enjoy it much, and exprefs their eagernefs by barking every time they raife their heads above the water to breathe. The net is held by two In-dians, who get into the water; then the dogs, taking a large compafs, dive after the fifh, and drive them into the net; but it is only in particular places that the fifh are taken in this manner. At the clofe of the evening, the women

brought

brought in two fifh, which ferved us for fupper ; and then we repofed ourfelves as before. Here we remained all the next day ; and the morning after embarked again, and rowed till noon ; then landing, we defcried the canoes of the Indian men, who had been fome time expected from an expedition they had been upon. This was foon to make a great alteration in the fituation of my affairs, a prefage of which I could read in the melancholy countenance of my young hoftefs. She endeavoured to exprefs herfelf in very earneft terms to me ; but I had not yet acquired a competent knowledge of the Indian language to underftand her.

As foon as the men were landed, fhe and the old Indian woman went up, not without fome marks of dread upon them, to an elderly Indian man, whofe remarkable furly and ftern countenance was well calculated to raife fuch fenfa-

K 4   tions

tions in his dependents. He feemed to be a cacique, or chief man among them, by the airs of importance he affumed to himfelf, and the deference paid him by the reft. After fome little conference paffed between thefe Indians, and our cacique conductor, of which, moft probably, the circumftances of our hiftory, and the occafion of our coming here, might be the chief fubject; for they fixed their eyes conftantly upon us, they applied themfelves to building their wigwams. I now underftood that the two Indian women with whom I had fojourned, were wives to this chieftain, though one was young enough to be his daughter; and as far as I could learn, did really ftand in the different relations to him both of daughter and wife. It was eafy to be perceived that all did not go well between them at this time; either that he was not fatisfied with the anfwers that they returned him to his queftions,

queſtions, or that he ſuſpected ſome miſ-
conduct on their ſide ; for preſently
after, breaking out into ſavage fury, he
took the young one up in his arms, and
threw her with violence againſt the
ſtones ; but his brutal reſentment did
not ſtop here, he beat her afterwards
in a cruel manner. I could not ſee this
treatment of my benefactreſs without
the higheſt concern for her, and rage
againſt the author of it ; eſpecially as
the natural jealouſy of theſe people gave
occaſion to think that it was on my account ſhe ſuffered. I could hardly ſup-
preſs the firſt emotions of my reſentment,
which prompted me to return him his
barbarity in his own kind ; but beſides
that this might have drawn upon her
freſh marks of his ſeverity, it was neither politic, nor indeed in my power, to
have done it to any good purpoſe at this
time.

Our

Our cacique now made us underftand that we muft embark directly,
in the fame canoe which brought us,
and return to our companions ; and that
the Indians we were about to leave,
would join us in a few days, when we
fhould all fet out in a body, in order to
proceed to the northward. In our way
back, nothing very material happened ;
but upon our arrival, which was the
next day, we found Mr. Elliot, the furgeon, in a very bad way ; his illnefs had
been continually increafing fince we left
him. Mr. Hamilton and Mr. Campbell
were almoft ftarved, having fared very ill
fince we left them : a few fea-eggs were
all the fubfiftence they had lived upon ;
and thefe procured by the cacique's wife,
in the manner I mentioned before. This
woman was the very reverfe of my
hoftefs ; and as fhe found her hufband
was of fo much confequence to us, took
upon

upon her with much haughtinefs, and treated us as dependents and flaves. He was not more engaging in his carriage towards us ; he would give no part of what he had to fpare to any but captain Cheap, whom his intereft led him to pre-fer to the reft, though our wants were often greater. The captain, on his part, con-tributed to keep us in this abject fitua-tion, by approving this diftinction the cacique fhewed to him. Had he treated us with not quite fo much diftance, the cacique might have been more regardful of our wants. The little regard and at-tention which our neceffitous condition drew from captain Cheap, may be im-puted likewife, in fome meafure, to the effects of a mind foured by a feries of croffes and difappointments ; which, in-deed, had operated on us all to a great neglect of each other, and fometimes of ourfelves.

We

We were not fuffered to be in the fame wigwam with the cacique and his wife; which, if we had had any countenance from captain Cheap, would not have been refufed. What we had made for ourfelves was in fuch a bungling manner, that it fcarce deferved the name even of this wretched fort of habitation. But our untoward circumftances now found fome relief in the arrival of the Indians we waited for; who brought with them fome feal, a fmall portion of which fell to our fhare. A night or two after they fent out fome of their young men, who procured us a quantity of a very delicate kind of birds, called fhags and cormorants. Their manner of taking thefe birds refembles fomething a fport called bat-fowling. They find out their haunts among the rocks and cliffs in the night, when taking with them torches made of the

bark

bark of the birch tree, which is common here, and grows to a very large fize (this bark has a very unctuous quality, and emits a bright and clear light; and in the northern parts of America is ufed frequently inftead of a candle) they bring the boat's fide as near as poffible to the rocks, under the roofting-places of thefe birds; then waving their lights backwards and forwards, the birds are dazzled and confounded fo as to fall into the canoe, where they are inftantly knocked on the head with a fhort ftick the Indians take with them for that pur-pofe.

Seal are taken in fome lefs frequented parts of thefe coafts, with great eafe; but when their haunts have been two or three times difturbed, they foon learn to provide for their fafety, by repairing to the water upon the firft alarm. This is the cafe with them hereabouts; but as they frequently raife their heads above

8   water

water, either to breathe or look about
them, I have feen an Indian at this interval, throw his lance with fuch dexterity as to ftrike the animal through
both its eyes, at a great diftance ; and it
is very feldom that they mifs their aim.

As we were wholly unacquainted with
thefe methods of providing food for ourfelves, and were without arms and ammunition, we were drove to the utmoft
ftraits ; and found ourfelves rather in
worfe condition than we had been at
any time before.   For the Indians, having now nothing to fear from us, we
found we had nothing to expect from
them upon any other motive.   Accordingly, if they ever did relieve us, it was
through caprice ; for at moft times they
would fhew themfelves unconcerned at
our greateft diftreffes.   But the good
Indian women, whofe friendfhip I had
experienced before, continued, from
time to time, their good offices to me.

Though

Though I was not fuffered to enter their wigwams, they would find opportunities of throwing in my way fuch fcraps as they could fecrete from their hufbands. The obligation I was under to them on this account is great, as the hazard they ran in conferring thefe favours was little lefs than death. The men, unreftrained by any laws or ties of confcience, in the management of their own families, exercife a moft defpotic authority over their wives, whom they confider in the fame view they do any other part of their property, and difpofe of them accordingly : even their common treatment of them is cruel ; for though the toil and hazard of procuring food lies entirely upon the women, yet they are not fuffered to touch any part of it till the hufband is fatisfied ; and then he affigns them their portion, which is generally very fcanty, and fuch as he has not a ftomach for himfelf.

6   This

This arbitrary proceeding, with refpect to their own families, is not peculiar to this people only. I have had occafion to obferve it in more inftances than this I have mentioned, among many other nations of favages I have fince feen.

Thefe Indians are of a middling ftature, well fet, and very active ; and make their way among the rocks with an amazing agility. Their feet, by this kind of exercife, contract a callofity which renders the ufe of fhoes quite un-neceffary to them. But before I conclude the few obfervations I have to make on a people fo confined in all their notions and practice, it may be expected I fhould fay fomething of their religion ; but as their grofs ignorance is in nothing more confpicuous, and as we found it advife-able to keep out of their way when the fits of devotion came upon them, which is rather frantic than religious, the reader can expect very little fatisfaction

on

on this head. Accident has fometimes
made me unavoidably a fpectator of
fcenes I fhould have chofen to have with-
drawn myfelf from; and fo far I am in-
ftructed. As there are no fixed feafons
for their religious exercifes, the younger
people wait till the elders find themfelves
devoutly difpofed; who begin the ceremony by feveral deep and difmal groans,
which rife gradually to a hideous kind
of finging, from which they proceed to
enthufiafm, and work themfelves into a
difpofition that borders on madnefs; for
fuddenly jumping up, they fnatch fire-
brands from the fire, put them in their
mouths, and run about burning every
body they come near: at other times, it
is a cuftom with them to wound one
another with fharp mufcle-fhells till
they are befmeared with blood. Thefe
orgies continue till thofe who prefide in
them foam at the mouth, grow faint, are
exhaufted with fatigue, and diffolve in a

L   profufion

profufion of fweat. When the men drop their part in this frenzy, the women take it up, acting over again much the fame kind of wild fcene, except that they rather outdo the men in fhrieks and noife. Our cacique, who had been reclaimed from thefe abominations by the Spaniards, and juft knew the exterior form of croffing himfelf, pretended to be much offended at thefe profane ceremonies, and that he would have died fooner than have partaken of them. Among other expreffions of his difapprobation, he declared, that whilft the favages folemnized thefe horrid rites, he never failed to hear ftrange and uncommon noifes in the woods, and to fee frightful vifions ; and affured us, that the devil was the chief actor among them upon thefe occafions.

It might be about the middle of March, that we embarked with thefe Indians. They feparated our little company intirely, not putting any two of us together

together in the same canoe. The oar was my lot, as usual, as also Mr. Campbell's; Mr. Hamilton could not row, and captain Cheap was out of the question; our surgeon was more dead than alive at the time, and lay at the bottom of the canoe he was in. The weather coming on too bad for their canoes to keep the sea, we landed again, without making great progress that day. Here Mr. Elliot, our surgeon, died. At our first setting out, he promised the fairest for holding out, being a very strong, active young man: he had gone through an infinite deal of fatigue, as Mr. Hamilton and he were the best shots amongst us, and whilst our ammunition lasted never spared themselves, and in a great measure provided for the rest; but he died the death many others had done before him, being quite starved. We scraped a hole for him in the sand, and buried him in the best manner we could.

Here

Here I muſt relate a little anecdote of our chriſtian cacique. He and his wife had gone off, at ſome diſtance from the ſhore, in their canoe, when ſhe dived for ſea-eggs; but not meeting with great ſuccefs, they returned a good deal out of humour. A little boy of theirs, about three years old, whom they appeared to be doatingly fond of, watching for his father and mother's return, ran into the ſurf to meet them: the father handed a baſket of ſea-eggs to the child, which being too heavy for him to carry, he let it fall; upon which the father jumped out of the canoe, and catching the boy up in his arms, daſhed him with the utmoſt violence againſt the ſtones. The poor little creature lay motionleſs and bleeding, and in that condition was taken up by the mother; but died ſoon after. She appeared inconſolable for ſome time; but the brute

his

his father ſhewed little concern about
it. A day or two after we put to ſea
again, and croſſed the great bay I mentioned we had been to the bottom of,
when we firſt hauled away to the weſtward. The land here was very low and
ſandy, with ſomething like the mouth of a
river which diſcharged itſelf into the ſea;
and which had been taken no notice of
by us before, as it was ſo ſhallow that
the Indians were obliged to take every
thing out of their canoes, and carry it
over the neck of land, and then haul the
boats over into a river, which at this
part of it was very broad, more reſem-
bling a lake than a river. We rowed up
it for four or five leagues, and then took
into a branch of it, that ran firſt to the
eaſtward, and then to the northward:
here it became much narrower, and the
ſtream exceſſively rapid, ſo that we made
but little way, though we worked very
hard. At night we landed upon its

banks,

banks, and had a moſt uncomfortable lodging, it being a perfect ſwamp ; and we had nothing to cover us, though it rained very hard. The Indians were little better off than we, as there was no wood here to make their wigwams.; ſo that all they could do was to prop up the bark they carry in the bottom of their canoes with their oars, and ſhelter themſelves as well as they could to leeward of it. They, knowing the difficulties that were to be encountered here, had provided themſelves with ſome ſeal ; but we had not the leaſt morſel to eat, after the heavy fatigues of the day, excepting a ſort of root we ſaw ſome of the Indians make uſe of, which was very diſagreeable to the taſte. We laboured all the next day againſt the ſtream, and fared as we had done the day before. The next day brought us to the carrying-place. Here was plenty of wood ; but nothing to be got for ſuſtenance.

nance. The firſt thing the Indians did was to take every thing out of their canoes; and after hauling them aſhore, they made their wigwams. We paſſed this night, as generally we had done, under a tree; but what we ſuffered at this time is not eaſily to be expreſſed. I had been three days at the oar without any kind of nouriſhment, but the wretched root I mentioned before. I had no ſhirt, as mine was rotted off by bits; and we were devoured by vermin. All my cloaths conſiſted of an old ſhort grieko, which is ſomething like a bearſkin, with a piece of a waiſtcoat under it, which once had been of red cloth, both which I had on when I was caſt away; I had a ragged pair of trowſers, without either ſhoe or ſtocking. The firſt thing the Indians did in the morning was to take their canoes to pieces: and here, for the information of the reader, it will be neceſſary to deſcribe the ſtructure of

theſe

thefe boats, which are extremely well calculated for the ufe of thefe Indians, as they are frequently obliged to carry them over land a long way together, through thick woods, to avoid doubling capes and headlands, in feas where no open boat·could live. They generally confift of five pieces, or planks ; one for the bottom, and two for each fide ; and as thefe people have no iron tools, the labour muft be great in hacking a fingle plank out of a large tree with fhells and flints, though with the help of fire. Along the edges of the plank, they make fmall holes, at about an inch from one to the other, and few them together with the fupple-jack, or woodbine ; but as thefe holes are not filled up by the fubftance of the woodbine, their boats would be immediately full of water if they had not a method of preventing it. They do this very effectually by the bark of a tree, which they firft fteep in water

for

for fome time, and then beat it between
two ftones till it anfwers the ufe of oak-
um, and then chinfe each hole fo well,
that they do not admit of the leaft water
coming through, and are eafily taken
afunder and put together again. When
they have occafion to go over land, as
at this time, each man or woman carries
a plank ; whereas it would be impoffible
for them to drag a heavy boat intire.
Every body had fomething to carry except captain Cheap; and he was obliged
to be affifted, or never would have got
over this march ; for a worfe than this,
I believe, never was made. He, with
the others, fet out fome time before me.
I waited for two Indians, who belonged
to the canoe I came in; and who remained to carry over the laft of the things
from the fide we were on. I had a
piece of wet heavy canvas, which belonged to captain Cheap, with a bit of ftinking
feal wrapped in it (which had been given
him

him that morning by fome of the Indians) to carry upon my head, which
was a fufficient weight for a ftrong man
in health, through fuch roads, and a
grievous burthen to one in my condition. Our way was through a thick
wood, the bottom of which was a mere
quagmire, moft part of it up to our
knees, and often to our middle, and every now and then we had a large tree to
get over ; for they often lay directly in
our road. Befides this, we were continually treading upon the ftumps of trees,
which were not to be avoided, as they
were covered with water; and having
neither fhoe nor ftocking, my feet and
legs were frequently torn and wounded.
Before I had got half a mile, the two Indians had left me ; and making the beft
of my way, left they fhould be all gone
before I got to the other fide, I fell off a
tree that croffed the road, into a very deep
fwamp, where I very narrowly efcaped
drowning,

drowning, by the weight of the burthen
I had on my head. It was a long while
before I could extricate myfelf from this
difficulty ; and when I did, my ftrength
was quite exhaufted. I fat down under
a tree, and there gave way to melancholy reflexions. However, as I was
fenfible thefe reflexions would anfwer
no end, they did not laft long. I got
up, and marking a great tree, I then depofited my load, not being able to carry
it any farther, and fet out to join my
company. It was fome hours before I
reached my companions. I found them
fitting under a tree, and fat myfelf
down by them without fpeaking a word;
nor did they fpeak to me, as I remember, for fome time ; when captain Cheap
breaking filence, began to afk after the
feal and piece of canvas. I told him the
difafter I had met with, which he might
have eafily gueffed by the condition the
rags I had on were in, as well as having
my

feet and ancles cut to pieces; but instead of compaffion for my fufferings,
I heard nothing but grumbling from
every one, for the irreparable lofs they
had fuftained by me. I made no anfwer;
but after refting myfelf a little, I got up
and ftruck into the wood, and walked
back at leaft five miles to the tree I had
marked, and returned juft time enough
to deliver it before my companions embarked, with the Indians, upon a great
lake, the oppofite part of which feemed
to wafh the foot of the Cordilleras. I
wanted to embark with them; but was
given to underftand I was to wait for
fome other Indians that were to follow
them. I knew not where thefe Indians
were to come from: I was left alone
upon the beach, and night was at hand.
They left me not even a morfel of the
ftinking feal that I had fuffered fo much
about. I kept my eyes upon the boats
as long as I could diftinguifh them; and
then

then returned into the wood, and fat myfelf down upon the root of a tree, having eat nothing the whole day but the ftem of a plant which refembles that of an artichoke, which is of a juicy confiftence, and acid tafte. Quite worn out with fatigue, I foon fell afleep; and awaking before day, I thought I heard fome voices at no great diftance from me. As the day appeared, looking further into the wood, I perceived a wigwam, and immediately made towards it; but the reception I met with was not at all agreeable; for ftooping to get into it, I prefently received two or three kicks in my face, and at the fame time heard the found of voices feemingly in anger; which made me retire, and wait at the foot of a tree, where I remained till an old woman peeped out, and made figns to me to draw near. I obeyed very readily, and went into the wigwam: in it were three men and two women; one

young

young man feemed to have great refpect
fhewn to him by the reft, though he was
the moft miferable object I ever faw. He
was a perfect fkeleton, and covered with
fores from head to foot. I was happy
to fit a moment by their fire, as I was
quite benumbed with cold. The old
woman took out a piece of feal, holding
one part of it between her feet, and the
other end in her teeth, and then cut off
fome thin flices with a fharp fhell, and
diftributed them about to the other Indians. She then put a bit on the fire,
taking a piece of fat in her mouth, which
fhe kept chewing, every now and then
fpirting fome of it on the piece that was
warming upon the fire ; for they never
do more with it than warm it through.
When it was ready, fhe gave me a little
bit, which I fwallowed whole, being almoft ftarved. As thefe Indians were all
ftrangers to me, I did not know which
way they were going ; and indeed it was
now

now become quite indifferent to me
which way I went, whether to the northward or fouthward, fo that they would
but take me with them, and give me
fomething to eat. However, to make
them comprehend me, I pointed firft to
the fouthward, and after to the lake, and
I foon underftood they were going to the
northward. They all went out together,
excepting the fick Indian, and took up
the plank of the canoe, which lay near
the wigwam, and carried it upon the
beach, and prefently put it together ; and
getting every thing into it, they put me
to the oar. We rowed acrofs the lake
to the mouth of a very rapid river, where
we put afhore for that night, not daring
to get any way down in the dark ; as it
required the greateft fkill, even in the
day, to avoid running foul of the ftumps
and roots of trees, of which this river
was full. I paffed a melancholy night,
as they would not fuffer me to come

near

near the wigwam they had made; nor did they give me the leaſt bit of any one thing to eat ſince we embarked. In the morning we ſet off again. The weather proved extremely bad the whole day. We went down the river at an amazing rate; and juſt before night they put aſhore upon a ſtony beach. They hauled the canoe up, and all diſappeared in a moment, and I was left quite alone: it rained violently, and was very dark. I thought it was as well to lay down upon the beach, half ſide in water, as to get into a ſwamp under a dropping tree. In this diſmal ſituation I fell aſleep, and awaked three or four hours after in ſuch agonies with the cramp, that I thought I muſt die upon the ſpot. I attempted ſeveral times to raiſe myſelf upon my legs, but could not. At laſt I made ſhift to get upon my knees, and looking towards the wood I ſaw a great fire at ſome diſtance from me. I was a long time

6   crawling

crawling to it ; and when I reached it, I threw myfelf almoft into it, in hopes of finding fome relief from the pain I fuffered. This intrufion gave great offence to the Indians, who immediately got up, kicking and beating me till they drove me to fome diftance from it ; however, I contrived, a little after, to place myfelf fo as to receive fome warmth from it; by which I got rid of the cramp. In the morning we left this place, and were foon after out of the river. Being now at fea again, the Indians intended putting afhore at the firft convenient place, to look for fhell-fifh, their ftock of provifions having been quite exhaufted for fome time. At low water we landed upon a fpot that feemed to promife well ; and here we found plenty of limpets. Though at this time ftarving, I did not attempt to eat one, left I fhould lofe a moment in gathering them ; not knowing how foon the Indians might be going again. I had

M   almoft

almoſt filled my hat when I ſaw them returning to the canoe. I made what haſte I could to her; for I believe they would have made no conſcience of leaving me behind. I ſat down to my oar again, placing my hat cloſe to me, every now and then eating a limpet. The Indians were employed the ſame way, when one of them ſeeing me throw the ſhells overboard, ſpoke to the reſt in a violent paſſion; and getting up, fell upon me, and ſeizing me by an old ragged handkerchief I had about my neck, almoſt throttled me; whilſt another took me by the legs, and was going to throw me overboard, if the old woman had not prevented them. I was all this time intirely ignorant by what means I had given offence, till I obſerved that the Indians, after eating the limpets, carefully put the ſhells in a heap at the bottom of the canoe. I then concluded there was ſome ſuperſtition about throwing

theſe

thefe fhells into the fea, my ignorance of
which had very nearly coft me my life.
I was refolved to eat no more limpets till
we landed, which we did fome time after, upon an ifland. I then took notice
that the Indians brought all their fhells
afhore, and laid them above high water
mark. Here, as I was going to eat a
large bunch of berries I had gathered
from a tree, for they looked very tempt-
ing, one of the Indians fnatched them out
of my hand and threw them away,
making me to underftand that they were
poifonous. Thus, in all probability, did
thefe people now fave my life, who, a
few hours before, were going to take it
from me for throwing away a fhell.

In two days after, I joined my companions again ; but don't remember
that there was the leaft joy fhewn on either fide at meeting. At this place was
a very large canoe belonging to our
guide, which would have required at

leaft fix men to the oar to have made any
kind of expedition: inftead of that, there
was only Campbel and myfelf, befides
the Indian, his companion, or fervant, to
row, the cacique himfelf never touching
an oar, but fitting with his wife all the
time much at his eafe. Mr. Hamilton
continued in the fame canoe he had been
in all along, and which ftill was to keep
us company fome way further, though
many of the others had left us. This
was dreadful hard work to fuch poor
ftarved wretches as we were, to be flav-
ing at the oar all day long in fuch a
heavy boat; and this inhuman fellow
would never give us a fcrap to eat, excepting when he took fo much feal that
he could not contrive to carry it all away
with him, which happened very feldom.
After working like galley-flaves all day,
towards night, when we landed, inftead
of taking any reft, Mr. Campbell and I
were fometimes obliged to go miles

along

along fhore to get a few fhell-fifh; and
juft as we have made a little fire in order
to drefs them, he has commanded us into
the boat again, and kept us rowing the
whole night without ever landing. It
is impoffible for me to defcribe the miferable ftate we were reduced to our bodies were fo emaciated, that we hardly
appeared the figures of men. It has
often happened to me in the coldeft night,
both in hail and fnow, where we had
nothing but an open beach to lay down
upon, in order to procure a little reft,
that I have been obliged to pull off the
few rags I had on, as it was impoffible
to get a moment's fleep with them on for
the vermin that fwarmed about them;
though I ufed, as often as I had time,
to take my clothes off, and putting them
upon a large ftone, beat them with another, in hopes of killing hundreds at
once; for it was endlefs work to pick
them off. What we fuffered from this,

M 3   was

was ten times worfe even than hunger. But we were clean in comparifon to captain Cheap; for I could compare his body to nothing but an ant-hill, with thoufands of thofe infects crawling over it; for he was now paft attempting to rid himfelf in the leaft from this torment, as he had quite loft himfelf, not recollecting our names that were about him, or even his own. His beard was as long as a hermit's : that and his face being covered with train-oil and dirt, from having long accuftomed himfelf to fleep upon a bag, by the way of pillow, in which he kept the pieces of ftinking feal. This prudent method he took to prevent our getting at it whilft he flept. His legs were as big as mill-pofts, though his body appeared to be nothing but fkin and bone.

One day we fell in with about forty Indians, who came down to the beach we landed on, curioufly painted. Our ca-

cique

cique feemed to underftand but little of their language, and it founded to us very different from what we had heard before. However, they made us comprehend that a fhip had been upon the coaft not far from where we then were, and that fhe had a red flag: this we underftood fome time after to have been the Anne pink, whofe adventures are particularly related in Lord Anfon's Voyage; and we paffed through the very harbour fhe had lain in.

As there was but one fmall canoe that intended to accompany us any longer; and that in which Mr. Hamilton had been to this time, intended to proceed no further to the northward; our cacique propofed to him to come into our canoe, which he refufed, as the infolence of this fellow was to him infupportable; he therefore rather chofe to remain where he was, till chance fhould throw in his way fome other means of getting for-

M 4 ward:

ward fo here we left him ; and it was
fome months before we faw him again.

We now got on, by very flow degrees, to
the northward ; and as the difficulties and
hardfhips we daily went through would
only be a repetition of thofe already
mentioned, I fhall fay no more, but that
at laft we reached an ifland about thirty
leagues to the fouthward of Chiloe.
Here we remained two days for a favourable opportunity to crofs the bay, the very
thoughts of which feemed to frighten
our cacique out of his fenfes ; and indeed, there was great reafon for his apprehenfions ; for there ran a moft dreadful hollow fea, dangerous, indeed, for
any open boat whatever, but a thoufand
times more for fuch a crazy veffel as we
were in. He at length muftered up refolution enough to attempt it, firft having
croffed himfelf for an hour together, and
made a kind of lug-fail out of the bits of
blankets they wore about them, fewed
together

together with fplit fupple jacks. We
then put off, and a terrible paffage we
had. The bottom plank of the canoe
was fplit, which opened upon every fea ;
and the water continually rufhing over
the gunnel, I may fay that we were in
a manner full the whole way over,
though all hands were employed in baling without ceafing a moment. As we
drew near the fhore, the cacique was
eager to land, having been terrified to
that degree with this run, that if it had
not been for us, every foul muft have
perifhed ; for he had very near got in
amongft the breakers, where the fea drove
with fuch violence upon the rocks, that
not even an Indian could have efcaped,
efpecially as it was in the night. We
kept off till we got into fmooth water,
and landed upon the ifland of Chiloe;
though in a part of it that was not inhabited. Here we ftaid all the next day,
in a very heavy fnow, to recover ourfelves
a little

(170)

a little after our fatigue ; but the cold
was fo exceffive, having neither fhoe nor
ftocking, we thought we fhould have loft
our feet ; and captain Cheap was fo ill,
that if he had had but a few leagues
further to have gone without relief, he
could not have held out. It pleafed God
now that our fufferings, in a great meafure, were drawing to an end.

What things our cacique had brought
with him from the wreck, he here buried under ground, in order to conceal
them from the Spaniards, who would
not have left him a rufty nail if they
had known of it. Towards evening,
we fet off again ; and about nine the fame
night, to our great joy, we obferved
fomething that had the appearance of a
houfe. It belonged to an acquaintance
of our cacique ; and as he was poffeffed
of my fowling-piece, and we had preferved about one charge of powder, he
made us load it for him, and defired we

would

would fhew him how to difcharge it;
upon which, ftanding up, and holding
his head from it as far as poffible, he
fired, and fell back into the bottom of
the canoe. The Indians belonging to
the houfe, not in the leaft ufed to fire-
arms, ran out and hid themfelves in
the woods. But after fome time, one of
them, bolder than the reft, got upon a
hill, and hollowed to us, afking who and
what we were. Our cacique now made
himfelf known, and they prefently came
down to the boat, bringing with them
fome fifh, and plenty of potatoes. This
was the moft comfortable meal we had
made for many long months; and as
foon as this was over we rowed about
two miles farther to a little village,
where we landed. Here our cacique
prefently awaked all the inhabitants
by the noife he made, and obliged one
of them to open his door to us, and
immediately to make a large fire; for
the

the weather was very fevere, this being the month of June, the depth of winter in this part of the world. The Indians now flocked thick about us, and feemed to have great compaffion for us, as our cacique related to them what part he knew of our hiftory. They knew not what countrymen we were, nor could our guide inform them ; for he had often afked us if we were French, Dutch, or Englifh, the only nations he had ever heard of befides the Spaniards. We always anfwered we were from Grande Bretagne, which he could make nothing of ; for we were afraid, if he knew us to be Englifh, as he had heard that nation was at war with the Spaniards, he never would have conducted us to Chiloe.

Thefe good-natured compaffionate creatures feemed to vie with each other who fhould take the moft care of us. They made a bed of fheep-fkins clofe to the fire, for captain Cheap, and laid him

upon

upon it ; and indeed, had it not been for
the kind affiftance he now met with, he
could not have furvived three days
longer. Though it was now about
midnight, they went out and killed a
fheep, of which they made broth, and
baked a large cake of barley-meal. Any
body may imagine what a neat this was
to wretches who had not tafted a bit
of bread, or any wholefome diet, for
fuch a length of time. After we could
eat no longer, we went to fleep about the
fire, which the Indians took care to keep
up. In the morning, the women came
from far and near, each bringing with
her fomething. Almoft every one had
a pipkin in her hand, containing either
fowls or mutton made into broth, potatoes, eggs, or other eatables. We fell to
work as if we had eat nothing in the
night, and employed ourfelves fo for the
beft part of the day. In the evening,
the men filled our houfe, bringing with
them

them fome jars of a liquor they called
chicha, made of barley-meal, and not
very unlike our oat-ale in tafte, which
will intoxicate thofe who drink a fufficient quantity of it; for a little has no
effect. As foon as the drink was out, a
frefh fupply of victuals was brought in;
and in this manner we paffed the whole
time we remained with thefe hofpitable
Indians. They are a ftrong well made
people, extremely well featured, both
men and women, and vaftly neat in their
perfons. The mens drefs is called by
them a puncho, which is a fquare piece
of cloth, generally in ftripes of different
colours, with a flit in the middle of it
wide enough to let their heads through,
fo that it hangs on their fhoulders,
half of it falling before, and the other
behind them: under this they wear a
fhort kind of flannel fhirt without fleeves
or neck. They have wide-kneed
breeches, fomething like the Dutch
feamen,

feamen, and on their legs a fort of knit bufkins without any feet to them ; but never any fhoes. Their hair is always combed very fmooth, and tied very tight up in a great bunch clofe to the neck : fome wear a very neat hat of their own making, and others go without. The women wear a fhift like the mens fhirts, without fleeves ; and over it a fquare piece of cloth, which they faften before with a large filver pin, and a petticoat of different ftripes: they take as much care of their hair as the men ; and both have always a kind of fillet bound very tight about the forehead, and made faft behind: in fhort, thefe people are as cleanly as the feveral favage nations we had met with before were beaftly. Upon our firft coming here, they had difpatched a meffenger to the Spanifh corregidore at Caftro, a town a confiderable diftance from hence, to inform him of our arrival. At the

end

end of three days, this man returned
with an order to the chief caciques of
thefe Indians we were amongft, to carry
us directly to a certain place, where
there would be a party of foldiers to receive us. Thefe poor people now feemed
to be under great concern for us, hearing by the meffenger the preparations
that were making to receive us ; for they
ftand in vaft dread of the Spanifh foldiery. They were very defirous of
knowing what countrymen we were.
We told them we were Englifh; and at
that time at war with the Spaniards ;
upon which they appeared fonder of us
than ever ; and I verily believe, if they
durft, would have concealed us amongft
them, left we fhould come to any harm.
They are fo far from being in the Spanifh intereft, that they deteft the very
name of a Spaniard. And, indeed, I am
not furprifed at it ; for they are kept under fuch fubjection, and fuch a laborious
flavery,

flavery, by mere dint of hard ufage and punifhments, that it appears to me the moft abfurd thing in the world, that the Spaniards fhould rely upon thefe people for affiftance upon any emergency. We embarked in the evening, and it was night before we got to the place where we were to be delivered up to the Spanifh guard. We were met by three or four officers, and a number of foldiers, all with their fpados drawn, who furrounded us as if they had the moft formidable enemy to take charge of, inftead of three poor helplefs wretches, who, notwithftanding the good living we had met with amongft thefe kind Indians, could hardly fupport ourfelves. They carried us to the top of a hill, and there put us under a fhed; for it confifted of a thatched roof, without any fides or walls, being quite open; and here we were to lay upon the cold ground. All forts of people now came to ftare at us as

N a fight;

a fight; but the Indian women never came empty-handed; they always brought with them either fowls, mutton, or some kind of provision to us; so that we lived well enough. However, we found a very sensible difference between the treatment we had met with from the Indians, and what we now experienced from the Spaniards : With the former, we were quite at liberty to do as we pleased; but here, if we only went ten yards to attempt at getting rid of some of the vermin that devoured us, we had two soldiers, with drawn spados, to attend us. About the third day, a jesuit from Castro came to see us; not from a motive of compassion, but from a report spread by our Indian cacique, that we had some things of great value about us. Having by chance seen captain Cheap pull out a gold repeating watch, the first thing the good father did was to lug out of his pocket a bottle of brandy, and give

us

us a dram, in order to open our hearts.
He then came roundly to the point, afking us if we had faved no watches or
rings. Captain Cheap declared he had
nothing, never fufpecting that the Indian had feen his watch, having, as he
thought, always taken great care to conceal it from him ; but knowing that
Campbel had a filver watch, which had
been the property of our furgeon, he
defired him to make it a prefent to the
jefuit, telling him, at the fame time, that
as thefe people had great power and
authority, it might be of fervice to us
hereafter. This Campbel very unwil-
lingly did, and received from the father,
not long after, a pitiful prefent, not a
quarter part of the value of the rim of the
watch. We underftood afterwards, that
this had come to the governor's ears, who
was highly offended at it, as thinking
that if any thing of that fort had been
to be had, it was his due ; and did not

N 2   fpare

fpare the jefuits in the leaft upon the occafion. Soon after this, the officer of the guard informed us there was an or-der come to carry us to Caftro. In the evening, we were conducted to the wa-ter-fide, and put into a large periago ; and there were feveral more, to attend us full of foldiers. About eight o'clock at night, we were off the town. The boats all laid upon their oars, and there was a great deal of ceremony ufed in hailing and afking for the keys, as if it had been a regular fortification. After fome time, we landed ; but could fee neither gates nor walls, nor any thing that had the appearance of a garrifon. As we walked up a fteep hill into the town, the way was lined with men who had broomfticks upon their fhoulders inftead of mufquets, and a lighted match in their hands. When we came to the corregidore's houfe, we found it full of people. He was an old man, very tall, with

with a long cloak on, a tye wig without
any curl, and a fpado of immenfe length
by his fide. He received us in great
ftate and form ; but as we had no inter-
preter, we underftood little or nothing of
the queftions he afked us. He ordered
a table to be fpread for us with cold
ham and fowls ; which we three only fat
down to, and in a fhort time difpatched
more than ten men with common appe-
tites would have done. It is amazing,
that our eating to that excefs we had
done, from the time we firft got amongft
thefe kind Indians, had not killed us ;
we were never fatisfied, and ufed to take
all opportunities, for fome months after,
of filling our pockets when we were not
feen, that we might get up two or three times
in the night to cram ourfelves. Captain
Cheap ufed to declare, that he was quite
afhamed of himfelf. After fupper, the
corregidore carried us to the jefuits college, attended by the foldiers, and all the

N 3   rabble

rabble of the town. This was intended, at prefent, for our prifon, till orders were received from the governor, who refided at Chaco, above thirty leagues from this place. When we got to the college, the corregidore defired the father provincial, as they ftiled him, or head of the jefuits here, to find out what religion we were of, or whether we had any or not. He then retired, the gates were fhut, and we were conducted to a cell. We found in it fomething like beds fpread on the floor, and an old ragged fhirt apiece, but clean, which was of infinite fervice to us ; nor did eating at firft give me half the fatisfaction this treafure of an old fhirt did. Though this college was large, there were but four jefuits in it, nor were there any more of that order upon the ifland. In the morning, captain Cheap was fent for by the father provincial : their converfation was carried on in Latin, perhaps not the

beft on either fide ; however, they made
fhift to underftand one another. When
he returned, he told us the good fathers
were ftill harping upon what things of
value we might have faved and concealed about us ; and that if we had any
thing of that fort, we could not do better
than let them have it. Religion feemed
to be quite out of the queftion at prefent ;
but a day or two after the corregidore being
informed that we were heretics, he defired
thefe jefuits would convert us ; but one of
them told him it was a mere joke to attempt it, as we could have no inducement upon that ifland to change our
religion ; but that when we got to Chili,
in fuch a delightful country as that was,
where there was nothing but diverfions
and amufements, we fhould be converted
faft enough. We kept clofe to our cell
till the bell rang for dinner, when we
were conducted into a hall, where there
was one table for the fathers, and an-

other

other for us. After a very long Latin prayer, we fat down and eat what was put before us, without a fingle word paffing at either table. As foon as we had finifhed, there was another long prayer, which, however, did not appear fo tedious as the firft; and then we retired to our cell again. In this manner we paffed eight days without ever ftirring out; all which time one might have imagined one's-felf out of the world; for excepting the bell for dinner, a filence reigned throughout the whole, as if the place had been uninhabited. A little before dark, on the eighth evening, we heard a violent knocking at the gate; which was no fooner opened than there entered a young officer booted and fpurred, who acquainted the fathers that he was fent by the governor to conduct us to Chaco. This young man was the governor's fon ; by which means he obtained a commiffion next in authority,

upon

upon this ifland, to his father. He
ought to have been kept at fchool; for he
was a vain, empty coxcomb, much dif-
liked by the people of the ifland. After
taking leave of the jefuits, who I imagine were not forry to be rid of us,
after finding their expectations baulked,
we fet out, having about thirty foldiers
on horfeback to attend us. We rode
about eight miles that night, when we
came to an Eftancia, or farm-houfe, belonging to an old lady, who had two
handfome daughters. Here we were very
well entertained; and the good old lady
feemed to have great compaffion for us.
She afked the governor's fon if he
thought his father would have any objection to my paffing a month with her
at her farm. As fhe was a perfon of
rank in this ifland, he faid he would acquaint his father with her requeft, and
made no doubt but he would grant it.
I obferved our foldiers, when they came

into

into the houfe, had none of them any
fhoes on, but wore bufkins, like the Indians, without any feet to them. They
all had monftrous great fpurs, fome of
filver and others of copper, which made
a rattling when they walked, like chains.
They were all ftout, ftrong-looking
men, as the Spaniards, natives of the
ifland, in general are. After a good
fupper, we had fheep-fkins laid near the
fire for us to fleep on. Early in the
morning we mounted again; and after
riding fome miles acrofs the country,
we came to the water-fide, where we
found feveral periagos waiting for us,
with fome officers in them. Moft of the
foldiers difmounted and embarked with
us, a few only being fent round with the
horfes. It was three days before we
arrived at Chaco, as the tides between
this ifland and the main are fo rapid that
no boat can ftem them. The fame pre-
caution was taken here as at Caftro; we
                                    paffed

paffed through a whole lane of foldiers, armed as I mentioned thofe to have been before, excepting a few, who really had matchlocks, the only fire arms they have here. The foldiers, upon our journey, had given a pompous account of el Palacio del Rey, or the king's palace, as they ftiled the governor's houfe, and therefore we expected to fee fomething very magnificent; but it was nothing better than a large thatched barn, partitioned off into feveral rooms. The governor was fitting at a large table covered with a piece of red ferge, having all the principal officers about him. After fome time, he made us fit down, attempting to converfe with us by his linguift, who was a ftupid old fellow, that could neither talk Englifh nor Spanifh, but faid he was born in England, had refided above forty years in that country, and having formerly been a buccaneer, was taken by the Spaniards

near

near Panama. The governor kept us to
fupper, and then we were conducted
acrofs the court to our apartment, which
was a place that had ferved to keep the
fire wood for the governor's kitchen;
however, as it was dry over head, we
thought ourfelves extremely well lodged.
There was a foldier placed at the door
with a drawn fpado in his hand, to prevent our ftirring out; which was quite
unneceffary, as we knew not where to
go if we had been at liberty. One of
thefe foldiers took a great fancy to my
ragged grieko, which had ftill fome
thoufands about it; and in exchange
gave me an old puncho, the fort of garment with a hole in the middle to put
one's head through, as above related to
be worn by the Indians; and for the little
bit of my waiftcoat that remained, he
gave me a pair of breeches. I now fhould
have thought myfelf very handfomely
equipped, if I had had but another fhirt.

2   The

The next day, about noon, the governor
fent for us, and we dined at his table; after
which we returned to our lodging, where
we were never alone; for every body
was curious to fee us. We paffed about
a week in this manner, when the centinel was taken off, and we were allowed
to look about us a little, though not to
go out of the palace, as they were pleafed
to call it. We dined every day with the
governor; but were not very fond of his
faft days, which fucceeded each other too
quickly. I contrived to make friends
with his fteward and cook; by which
means I always carried my pockets full
to my apartment, where I paffed my
time very agreeably. Soon after, we had
leave to walk about the town, or go
wherever we pleafed. Every houfe was
open to us; and though it was but an
hour after we had dined, they always
fpread a table, thinking we never could
eat enough after what we had fuffered;

and

and we were much of the fame opinion. They are, in general, a charitable, good fort of people; but very ignorant, and governed by their priefts, who make them belive juft what they pleafe. The Indian language is chiefly fpoken here, even by the Spaniards one amongft another; and they fay they think it a finer language than their own. The women have fine complexions, and many of them are very handfome; they have good voices, and can ftrum a little upon the guittar; but they have an ugly cuftom of fmoking tobacco, which is a very fcarce commodity here; and therefore is looked upon as a great treat when they meet at one another's houfes. The lady of the houfe comes in with a large wooden pipe crammed with tobacco; and after taking two or three hearty whiffs, fhe holds her head under her cloak left any of the fmoke fhould efcape, and then fwallows it; fome time after

you

you fee it coming out of her nofe and ears. She then hands the pipe to the next lady, who does the fame, till it has gone through the whole company. Their houfes are but very mean, as will be eafily imagined by what I have faid of the governor's. They make their fire in the middle of their rooms ; but have no chimneys ; there is a fmall hole at each end of the roof, to let the fmoke out. It is only the better fort of people that eat bread made of wheat, as they grow but very little here, and they have no mills to grind it ; but then they have great plenty of the fineft potatoes in the world : thefe are always roafted in the afhes, then fcraped, and ferved up at meals inftead of bread. They breed abundance of fwine, as they fupply both Chili and Peru with hams. They are in no want of fheep, but are not overftocked with cows ; owing, in a great meafure, to their own indolence in not clearing-away

i   the

the woods; which if they would be at
the pains to do, they might have suffi-
cient pasture. Their trade consists in
hams, hogs-lard, which is used throughout all South America instead of butter,
cedar plank, which the Indians are continually employed in cutting quite to the
foot of the Cordilleras, little carved boxes,
which the Spanish ladies use to put their
work in, carpets, quilts, and punchos
neatly embroidered all round; for these,
both in Chili and Peru, are used by the
people of the first fashion, as well as the
inferior sort, by way of riding-dress, and
are esteemed to be much more convenient
for a horseman than any kind of coat
whatever.

They have what they call an annual
ship from Lima, as they never expect
more than one in the year; though
sometimes it happens that two have
come, and at other times they have been
two or three years without any. When
this

this happens, they are greatly diftreffed, as this fhip brings them baize, cloth, linens, hats, ribbons, tobacco, fugar, brandy, and wine; but this latter article is chiefly for the ufe of the churches: matte, an herb from Paraguay, ufed all over South America inftead of tea, is alfo a neceffary article. This fhip's cargo is chiefly configned to the jefuits, who have more Indians employed for them than all the reft of the inhabitants together, and of courfe engrofs almoft the whole trade. There is no money current in this ifland. If any perfon wants a few yards of linen, a little fugar, tobacco, or any other thing brought from Peru, he gives fo many cedar-planks, hams, or punchos, in exchange. Some time after we had been here, a fnow arrived in the harbour from Lima, which occafioned great joy amongft the inhabitants, as they had no fhip the year before, from the alarm lord Anfon had

O   given

given upon the coaſt. This was not the annual veſſel, but one of thoſe that I mentioned before which come unexpectedly. The captain of her was an old man, well known upon the iſland, who had traded here once in two or three years, for more than thirty years paſt. He had a remarkable large head, and therefore was commonly known by a nick-name they had given him of Cabuço de Toro, or Bull's-head. He had not been here a week before he came to the governor, and told him, with a moſt melancholy countenance, that he had not ſlept a wink ſince he came into the harbour, as the governor was pleaſed to allow three Engliſh priſoners liberty to walk about inſtead of confining them; and that he expected every moment they would board his veſſel, and carry her away : this he ſaid when he had above thirty hands aboard. The governor aſſured him he would be anſwerable for

us,

us, and that he might sleep in quiet;
though at the same time he could not
help laughing at the man, as all the people in the town did. These assurances
did not satisfy the captain: he used the
utmost dispatch in disposing of his cargo,
and put to sea again, not thinking himself safe till he had lost sight of the
island. It was about three months after
us that Mr. Hamilton was brought in,
by a party that the governor had sent to
the southward on purpose to fetch him.
He was in a wretched condition upon his
first arrival, but soon recovered with the
good living he found here.

It is usual for the governor to make
a tour, every year, through the several
districts belonging to his government:
on this occasion he took us with him.
The first place he visited was Carelmapo,
on the main; and from thence to Castro.
At these places, he holds a kind of court;
all the chief caciques meeting him, and

informing

informing him of what has paffed fince
his laft vifit, and receiving frefh orders
for the year to come. At Caftro we had
the fame liberty we enjoyed at Chaco,
and vifited every body. It feemed they
had forgot all the ceremony ufed upon our
firft landing here, which was with an intent to make us believe it was ftrongly
fortified; for now they let us fee plainly
that they had neither fort nor gun. At
Chaco they had a little earthen fort,
with a fmall ditch palifadoed round it,
and a few old honey-combed guns without carriages, and which do not defend
the harbour in the leaft. Whilft we were
at Caftro, the old lady (at whofe houfe
we lay the firft night upon leaving the
jefuits college) fent to the governor, and
begged I might be allowed to come to
her for a few weeks : this was granted ;
and accordingly I went and paffed about
three weeks with her very happily, as
fhe feemed to be as fond of me as if I
had

had been her own fon. She was very
unwilling to part with me again; but
as the governor was foon to return to
Chaco, he fent for me, and I left my be-
nefactrefs with regret.

Amongft the houfes we vifited at
Caftro, there was one belonging to an old
prieft, who was efteemed one of the
richeft perfons upon the ifland. He had
a niece, of whom he was extremely fond,
and who was to inherit all he poffeffed.
He had taken a great deal of pains with
her education, and fhe was reckoned one
of the moft accomplifhed young ladies of
Chiloe. Her perfon was good, though
fhe could not be called a regular beauty.
This young lady did me the honour to
take more notice of me than I deferved,
and propofed to her uncle to convert me,
and afterwards begged his confent to
marry me. As the old man doated upon her, he readily agreed to it; and accordingly on the next vifit I made him, ac-

quainted

quainted me with the young lady's propofal, and his approbation of it, taking me at
the fame time into a room where there
were feveral chefts and boxes, which he
unlocked ; firft fhewing me what a number of fine cloaths his niece had, and
then his own wardrobe, which he faid
fhould be mine at his death. Amongft
other things, he produced a piece of
linen, which he faid fhould immediately be made up into fhirts for me. I
own this laft article was a great temptation to me ; however, I had the refolution
to withftand it, and made the beft excufes
I could for not accepting of the honour
they intended me ; for by this time I
could fpeak Spanifh well enough to make
myfelf underftood.

Amongft the Indians who had come to
meet the governor here, there were fome
caciques of thofe Indians who had treated
us fo kindly at our firft landing upon
Chiloe. One of thefe, a young man, had
been

been guilty of fome offence, and was put
in irons, and threatened to be more feverely
punifhed. We could not learn his crime,
or whether the governor did not do it in
a great meafure to fhew us his power
over thefe Indian chiefs : however, we
were under great concern for this young
man, who had been extremely kind to
us, and begged captain Cheap to inter-
cede with the governor for him. This
he did, and the cacique was releafed ; the
governor acquainting him at the fame
time, with great warmth, that it was to us
only he owed it, or otherwife he would
have made a fevere example of him. The
young man feemed to have been in no
dread of farther punifhment, as I believe
he felt all a man could do from the in-
dignity of being put in irons in the public fquare, before all his brother-ca-
ciques and many hundreds of other Indians. I thought this was not a very politic ftep of the governor, as the cacique

came

came after to captain Cheap to thank
him for his goodnefs, and in all probability would remember the Englifh for
fome time after; and not only he, but all
the other caciques who had been wit-
neffes of it, and who feemed to feel, if
poffible, even more than the young man
himfelf did. We now returned to Chaco,
and the governor told us, when the annual fhip came, which they expected in
December, we fhould be fent in her to
Chili. We felt feveral earthquakes
while we were here. One day as I happened to be upon a vifit at a houfe where
I was very well acquainted, an Indian
came in, who lived at many leagues diftance from this town, and who had made
this journey in order to purchafe fome
little trifles he wanted ; amongft other
things, he had bought fome prints of
faints. Very proud of thefe, he produced them, and put them into the hands
of the women, who very devoutly firft
croffed

croffed themfelves with them, and afterwards kiffed them ; then gave them to
me, faying at the fame time, they fuppofed fuch a heretic as I was would re-
fufe to kifs them. They were right in
their conjectures: I returned them to the
Indian without going through that ceremony. At that very inftant, there happened a violent fhock of an earthquake,
which they imputed intirely to the anger
of the faints ; and all quitted the houfe
as faft as they could, left it fhould fall
upon their heads. For my part, I made
the beft of my way home for fear of being knocked on the head, when out of the
houfe, by the rabble, who looked on me
as the caufe of all this mifchief, and did
not return to that houfe again till I
thought this affair was forgotten.

Here is a very good harbour ; but the
entrance is very dangerous for thofe who
are unacquainted with it, as the tides
are fo extremely rapid, and there are

funken

funken rocks in the mid-channel. The ifland is above feventy leagues round ; and the body of it lies in about 40 deg. 20 min. fouth, and is the moft fouthern fettlement the Spaniards have in thefe feas. Their fummer is of no long duration, and moft of the year round they have hard gales of wind and much rain. Oppofite the ifland, upon the Cordilleras, there is a volcano, which, at times, burns with great fury, and is fubject to violent eruptions. One of thefe alarmed the whole ifland, whilft we were here: it founded in the night like great guns. In the morning, the governor mounted his horfe, and rode backwards and forwards from his houfe to the earthen fort, faying it was the Englifh coming in, but that he would give them a warm reception ; meaning, I fuppofe, that he would have left them a good fire in his houfe; for I am certain he would foon have been in the woods, if

he

he had feen any thing like an Englifh
fhip coming in.

Women of the firft fafhion here feldom wear fhoes or ftockings in the
houfe, but only keep them to wear
upon particular occafions. I have often
feen them coming to the church, which
ftood oppofite to the governor's houfe,
bare-legg'd, walking through mud and
water; and at the church door put on
their fhoes and ftockings, and pull them
off again when they came out. Though
they are in general handfome, and
have good complexions, yet many of
them paint in fo ridiculous a manner,
that it is impoffible to help laughing in
their faces when you fee them.

The governor we found here was a
native of Chili. The government, which
is appointed by that prefidency, is for
three years; which appears to be a long
banifhment to them, as their appoint-
ments are but fmall, though they make
the

the moft of it. The towns of Caftro and Chaco confift only of fcattered houfes, without a regular ftreet ; though both have their places, or fquares, as almoft all Spanifh towns have. Chaco is very thinly inhabited, excepting at the time the Lima fhip arrives ; then they flock thither from all parts of the ifland, to purchafe what little matters they want ; and as foon as that is done, retire to their eftancias, or farms. It was about the middle of December this fhip came in ; and the fecond of January, 1742-3, we embarked on board of her. She was bound to Valparaifo. We got out to fea with fome difficulty, having been driven by the ftrength of the tide very near thofe funken rocks mentioned before. We found a great fea without ; and as the fhip was as deep as any laden collier, her decks were continually well wafhed. She was a fine veffel, of about two hundred and fifty tons. The timber the fhips of this country are built

of

lose so much money by it. The Indians

seamen for that climate. We had on

board the head of the jesuits as passenger.

He and captain Cheap were admitted

into the great cabin, and messed with the

captain and his chaplain. As for us,

we were obliged to ruff it the whole pas-

sage; that is, when we were tired we

lay down upon the quarter-deck, in the

open

open air, and flept as well as we could; but that was nothing to us, who had been ufed to fare fo much worfe. We lived well, eating with the mafter and boat-fwain, who always had their meals upon the quarter-deck, and drank brandy at them as we do fmall beer; and all the reft of the day were fmoaking fegars.

The fifth day we made the land four or five leagues to the fouthward of Val-paraifo; and foon after falling calm, a great weftern fwell hurried us in very faft towards the fhore. We dropped the lead feveral times, but had fuch deep water we could not anchor. They were all much alarmed when the jefuit came out of the cabin for the firft time, having been fea-fick the whole paffage. As foon as he was informed of the danger, he went back into the cabin, and brought out the image of fome faint, which he defired might be hung up in the mizen-fhrouds; which being done, he kept threat-

8   ening

ening it, that if we had not a breeze of wind soon, he would certainly throw it overboard. Soon after, we had a little wind from off the land, when the jesuit carried the image back with an air of great triumph, saying he was certain that we should not be without wind long, though he had given himself over for loft some time before it came. Next morning we anchored in the port of Val-paraiso. In that part which is oppofite to the fort, ships lay fo near the land, that they have generally three anchors ashore, as there is eight or ten fathom clofe to it; and the flaws come off the hills with fuch violence, that if it was not for this method of fecuring them, they would be blown out. This is only in fummer time, for in the winter months no ships ever attempt to come in here ; the northerly winds then prevail, and drive in fuch a fea that they muft foon be ashore.

The

The Spanifh captain waited upon the
governor of the fort, and informed him
that he had four Englifh prifoners on
board. We were ordered afhore in the
afternoon, and were received as we got
upon the beach, by a file of foldiers, with
their bayonets fixed, who furrounded us,
and then marched up to the fort, attended
by a numerous mob. We were carried
before the governor, whofe houfe was
full of officers. He was blind, afked a
few queftions, and then fpoke of nothing
but the ftrength of the garrifon he commanded, and defired to know if we had
obferved that all the lower battery was
brafs guns. We were immediately after, by his order, put into the condemned hole. There was nothing but
four bare walls, excepting a heap of lime
that filled one third of it, and made the
place fwarm with fleas in fuch a manner
that we were prefently covered with
them. Some of admiral Pizarro's foldiers

diers were here in garrifon that had been
landed from his fhips at Buenos Ayres,
as he could not get round Cape Horn.
A centinel's box was placed at our door,
and we had always a foldier with his
bayonet fixed, to prevent our ftirring
out. The curiofity of the people was
fuch, that our prifon was continually
full from morning till night, by which
the foldiers made a pretty penny, as they
took money from every perfon for the
fight. In a few days, captain Cheap
and Mr. Hamilton were ordered up to
St. Jago, as they were known to be officers by having faved their commiffions;
but Mr. Campbell and I were to continue
in prifon. Captain Cheap expreffed
great concern when he left us; he told
me it was what he had all along dreaded,
that they would feparate us when we
got into this country; but he affured
me, if he was permitted to fpeak to the
prefident, that he would never leave fol-

liciting him till he obtained a grant for
me to be fent up to him. No fooner
were they gone than we fared very badly.
A common foldier, who was ordered to
provide for us by the governor, brought
us each, once a day, a few potatoes
mixed with hot water. The other foldiers of the garrifon, as well as the
people who flocked to fee us, took notice
of it, and told the foldier it was cruel to
treat us in that manner. His anfwer
was, " The governor allows me but half a
real a day for each of thefe men ; what
can I do ? It is he that is to blame ; I
am fhocked every time I bring them this
fcanty pittance, though even that could
not be provided for the money he gives
them." We from this time lived much
better, and the foldier brought us even
wine and fruit. We took it for granted,
that our cafe had been reprefented to the
governor, and that he had increafed our
pay. As to the firft, we were right in
our

our conjectures ; it had been mentioned
to him, that it was impossible we could
subsist on what he allowed ; and his an-
swer to it was, that we might starve ; for
we should have no more from him, and
that he believed he should never be repaid
even that. This charitable speech of the
governor was made known every where,
and now almost every one who came to
see us gave us something ; even the
mule-drivers would take out their tobacco pouch, in which they kept their
money, and give us half a real. All
this we would have given to our soldier,
but he never would receive a farthing
from us, telling us we might still want
it ; and the whole time we were there,
which was some weeks, he laid aside
half his daily pay to supply us, though
he had a wife and six children, and
never could have the least hope or expectation of any recompence. However, two years after this, I had the sin-

gular

gular pleafure of making him fome return, when my circumftances were much
better than his. One night, when we
were locked up, there happened a dreadful fhock of an earthquake. We expected, every moment, the roof and
walls of our prifon to fall in upon us,
and crufh us to pieces ; and what added
to the horror of it was, the noife of
chains and imprecatións in the next prifon which joined to ours, where there
were near feventy felons heavily loaded
with irons, who are kept here to work
upon the fortifications, as in other countries they are condemned to the gallies.
A few days after this, we were told an
order was come from the prefident to
the governor to fend us up to St. Jago,
which is ninety miles from Valparaifo,
and is the capital of Chili. There were,
at this time, feveral fhips in the port
from Lima delivering their cargoes ; fo that
almoft every day there were large droves
of

of mules going up to St. Jago with the goods. The governor fent for one of the mafter-carriers, and ordered him to take us up with him. The man afked him how he was to be paid our expences, as he fhould be five days upon the road. The governor told him he might get that as he could, for he would not advance him a fingle farthing. After taking leave of our friendly foldier, who even now brought us fóme little matters to carry with us, we fet out, and travelled about fourteen miles the firft day, and lay at night in the open field, which is always the cuftom of thefe people, ftopping where there is plenty of pafture and good water for the mules. The next morning we paffed over a high mountain, called Zapata ; and then croffing a large plain, we paffed another mountain, very difficult for the mules, who each carried two heavy bales : there were above a hundred of them in this drove.

The

The mules of Chili are the fineſt in
the world ; and though they are continually upon the road, and have nothing
but what they pick up at nights, they
are as fat and ſleek as high-fed horſes in
England. The fourth night, we lay
upon a plain in ſight of St. Jago, and not
above four leagues from it. The next
day, as we moved towards the city, our
maſter-carrier, who was naturally well
diſpoſed, and had been very kind to us
all the way upon the road, adviſed me,
very ſeriouſly, not to think of remaining in St. Jago, where he ſaid there was
nothing but extravagance, vice, and folly,
but to proceed on with them as mule-
driver, which, he ſaid, I ſhould ſoon be
very expert at ; and that they led an
innocent and happy life, far preferable to
any enjoyment ſuch a great city as that
before us could afford. I thanked him,
and told him I was very much obliged
to him ; but that I would try the city firſt,
and

and if I did not like it, I would accept of the offer he was so good to make me. The thing that gave him this high opinion of me was, that as he had been so civil to us, I was very officious in assisting to drive in those mules that strayed from the rest upon those large plains we passed over; and this I thought was the least I could do towards making some returns for the obligations we were under to him.

When we got into St. Jago, the carrier delivered us to the captain of the guard, at the palace gate; and he soon after introduced us to the president, Don Joseph Manso, who received us very civilly, and then sent us to the house where captain Cheap and Mr. Hamilton were. We found them extremely well lodged at the house of a Scotch physician, whose name was don Patricio Gedd. This gentleman had been a long time in this city, and was greatly esteemed by the Spaniards, as

P 4 well

well for his abilities in his profeffion,
as his humane difpofition. He no
fooner heard that there were four Englifh
prifoners arrived in that country, than
he waited upon the prefident, and begged
they might be lodged at his houfe. This
was granted; and had we been his own
brothers, we could not have met with a
more friendly reception ; and during two
years that we were with him, his conftant ftudy was to make every thing as
agreeable to us as poffible. We were
greatly diftreffed to think of the expence
he was at upon our account ; but it was
in vain for us to argue with him about it.
In fhort, to fum up his character in a
few words, there never was a man of
more extenfive humanity. Two or three
days after our arrival, the prefident fent
Mr. Campbell and me an invitation to
dine with him, where we were to meet
admiral Pizarro and all his officers. This
was a cruel ftroke upon us, as we had not
any

any cloaths fit to appear in, and dared not refuse the invitation. The next day, a Spanish officer belonging to admiral Pizarro's squadron, whose name was don Manuel de Guiror, came and made us an offer of two thousand dollars. This generous Spaniard made this offer without any view of ever being repaid, but purely out of a compassionate motive of relieving us in our present distress. We returned him all the acknowledgments his uncommon generous behaviour merited, and accepted of six hundred dollars only, upon his receiving our draught for that sum upon the English consul at Lisbon. We now got ourselves decently cloathed after the Spanish fashion; and as we were upon our parole, we went out where we pleased to divert ourselves.

This city is situated in about 33 degrees and 30 minutes, south latitude, at the west foot of the immense chain of mountains called the Cordilleras. It stands

on

on a moft beautiful plain of above thirty leagues extent. It was founded by don Pedro de Baldivia, the conqueror of Chili. The plan of it was marked out by him in fquares, like Lima; and almoft every houfe belonging to people of any fafhion, has a large court before it, with great gates, and a garden behind. There is a little rivulet, neatly faced with ftone, runs through every ftreet; by which they can cool the ftreets, or water their gardens, when they pleafe. The whole town is extremely well paved. Their gardens are full of noble orange-trees and floripondies, with all forts of flowers, which perfume the houfes, and even the whole city. Much about the middle of it, is the great fquare, called the Plaça Real, or the Royal Square; there are eight avenues leading into it. The weft fide contains the cathedral and the bifhop's palace; the north fide is the prefident's palace, the royal court, the council houfe,

and

and the prifon; the fouth fide is a row of
piazzas, the whole length of which are
fhops, and over it a gallery to fee the
bull-feafts; the eaft fide has fome large
houfes belonging to people of diftinction;
and in the middle is a large fountain,
with a brafs bafon. The houfes have, in
general, only a ground floor, upon account of the frequent earthquakes; but
they make a handfome appearance. The
churches are rich in gilding, as well as
in plate: that of the jefuits is reckoned
an exceeding good piece of architecture;
but it is much too high built for a country fo fubject to earthquakes, and where
it has frequently happened that thoufands of people have been fwallowed up
at once. There is a hill, or rather high
rock, at the eaft end of the city, called
St. Lucia, from the top of which you
have a view of all the city, and the
country about for many leagues, afford-
ing a very delightful landfcape. Their
eftancias,

eftancias, or country houfes, are very
pleafant, having generally a fine grove of
olive trees, with large vineyards to them.
The Chili wine, in my opinion, is full
as good as Madeira, and made in fuch
quantities that it is fold extremely cheap.
The foil of this country is fo fertile, that
the hufbandmen have very little trouble;
for they do but in a manner fcratch up
the ground, and without any kind of
manure it yields an hundred fold. Without doubt the wheat of Chili is the fineft
in the woild, and the fruits arc all excellent in their kinds. Beef and mutton
are fo cheap, that you may have a good
cow for three dollars, and a fat fheep for
two fhillings. Their horfes are extraordinary good; and though fome of
them go at a great price, you may have
a very good one for four dollars, or
about eighteen fhillings of our money.
It muft be a very poor Indian who has
not his four or five horfes; and there are

no

no better horfemen in the world than
the Chileans; and that is not furprizing,
for they never chufe to go a hundred
yards on foot. They have always their
laço fixed to their faddle: the laço is a
long thong of leather, at the end of
which they make a fliding noofe. It is
of more general ufe to them than any
weapon whatever ; for with this they
are fure of catching either horfe or wild
bull, upon full gallop, by any foot they
pleafe. Their horfes are all trained to
this, and the moment they find the
thong ftraitened, as the other end is always made faft to the faddle, the horfe
immediately turns fhort, and throwing
the beaft thus caught, the huntfman
wounds or fecures him in what manner
he thinks proper. Thefe people are fo
dexterous, that they will take from the
ground a glove or handkerchief, while
their horfe is upon full ftretch ; and I
have feen them jump upon the back of
the

the wildeſt bull, and all the efforts of the
beaſt could not throw them. This country produces all ſorts of metals ; it is
famous for gold, ſilver, iron, tin, lead,
and quickſilver ; but ſome of theſe they
do not underſtand working, eſpecially
quickſilver. With copper they ſupply
all Peru, and ſend, likewiſe, a great deal
to Europe. The climate of Chili is, I
believe, the fineſt in the world. What
they call their winter does not laſt three
months ; and even that is very moderate,
as may be imagined by their manner
of building, for they have no chimneys
in their houſes. All the reſt of the year
is delightful ; for though from ten or
eleven in the morning till five in the
afternoon, it is very hot, yet the even-
ings and mornings are very cool and
pleaſant ; and in the hotteſt time of the
year, it is from ſix in the evening
till two or three in the morning, that
the people of this country meet to divert

vert themfelves with mufic and other en-
tertainments, at which there is plenty
of cooling liquors, as they are well fupplied with ice from the neighbouring
Cordilleras. At thefe affemblies, many
intrigues are carried on ; for they think
of nothing elfe throughout the year.
Their fandangoes are very agreeable ;
the women dance inimitably well, and
very gracefully. They are all born with
an ear for mufic, and moft of them
have delightful voices ; and all play
upon the guittar and harp. The latter,
at firft, appears a very aukward inftru-
ment for a woman ; yet that prejudice is
foon got over, and they far excel any
other nation upon it. They are extremely complaifant and polite ; and
when afked either to play, dance, or
fing, they do it without a moment's he-
fitation, and that with an exceeding good
grace. They have many·figure-dances ;
but what they take moft delight in, are
more

more like our hornpipes than any thing
elſe I can compare them to; and upon
theſe occaſions they ſhew ſurprizing activity. The women are remarkably
handſome, and very extravagant in their
dreſs. Their hair, which is as thick as
is poſſible to be conceived, they wear of
a vaſt length, without any other orna-
ment upon the head than a few flowers;
they plait it behind in four plaits, and
twiſt them round a bodkin, at each end
of which is a diamond roſe. Their
ſhifts are all over lace, as is a little tight
waiſtcoat they wear over them. Their
petticoats are open before, and lap over,
and have commonly three rows of very
rich lace of gold or ſilver. In winter,
they have an upper waiſtcoat of cloth of
gold or ſilver, and in ſummer, of the
fineſt linen, covered all over with the
fineſt Flanders lace. The ſleeves of theſe
are immenſely wide. Over all this,
when the air is cool, they have a mantle,

8   which

which is only of bays, of the fineſt colours, round which there is abundance
of lace. When they go abroad, they
wear a veil, which is ſo contrived that
one eye is only ſeen. Their feet are
very ſmall, and they value themſelves as
much upon it as the Chineſe do. Their
ſhoes are pinked and cut; their ſtock-
ings ſilk, with gold and ſilver clocks;
and they love to have the end of an
embroidered garter hang a little below
the petticoat. Their breaſts and ſhoul-
ders are very naked; and, indeed, you
may eaſily diſcern their whole ſhape by
their manner of dreſs. They have fine
ſparkling eyes, ready wit, a great deal
of good-nature, and a ſtrong diſpoſition
to gallantry.

By the deſcription of one houſe you
have an idea of all the reſt. You firſt
come into a large court, on one ſide of
which is the ſtable: you then enter a
hall; on one ſide of that is a large room,

about

about twenty feet wide, and near forty feet long: that fide next the window is the eftrado, which runs the whole length of the room. The eftrado is a platform, raifed about five or fix inches above the floor, and is covered with carpets and velvet cufhions for the women to fit on, which they do, after the Moorifh fafhion, crofs-legged. The chairs for the men are covered with printed leather. At the end of the eftrado, there is an alcove, where the bed ftands ; and there is always a vaft deal of the fheets hanging out, with a profufion of lace to them, and the fame on the pillows. They have a falfe door to the alcove, which fometimes is very convenient. Befides, there are generally two other rooms, one within another; and the kitchen and other offices are detached from the houfe, either at one fide or the end of the garden.

The

The ladies are fond of having
their Mulatto female flaves dreffed almoft as well as themfelves in every
refpect, excepting jewels, in which they
indulge themfelves to the utmoft extravagance. Paraguay tea, which they call
matte, as I mentioned before, is always
drunk twice à day : this is brought upon a large filver falver, with four legs
raifed upon it, to receive a little cup
made out of a fmall calabafh, or gourd,
and tipped with filver. They put the
herb firft into this, and add what fugar
they pleafe, and a little orange juice ; and
then pour hot water on them, and drink
it immediately, through the conveyance
of a long filver tube, at the end of
which there is a round ftrainer, to prevent the herb getting through. And
here it is reckoned a piece of politenefs
for the lady to fuck the tube two or
three times firft, and then give it the
ftranger to drink without wiping it.

They

They eat every thing so highly sea-
soned with red pepper, that those who
are not used to it, upon the first mouthful
would imagine their throats on fire for
an hour afterwards; and it is a common custom here, though you have the
greatest plenty at your own table, to
have two or three Mulatto girls come in
at the time you dine, bringing, in a little
silver plate, some of these high-seasoned
ragouts, with a compliment from Donna
such-a-one, who desires you will eat a
little bit of what she has sent you; which
must be done before her Mulatto's face,
or it would be deemed a great affront.
Had this been the fashion at Chiloe, we
should never have offended ; but sometimes here we could have wished this
ceremony omitted.

The president never asked any of us a
second time to his table. He expected us
once a fortnight to be at his levee, which
we never failed; and he always received

us

us very politely. He was a man of a
very amiable character, and much re-
fpected by every body in Chili, and
fome time after we left that country, was
appointed viceroy of Peru.

We had leave, whenever we afked it,
to make an excurfion into the country
for ten or twelve days at a time; which
we did fometimes to a very pleafant fpot
belonging to don Jofeph Dunofe, a
French gentleman, and a very fenfible,
well-bred man, who had married a very
agreeable lady at St. Jago, with a very
good fortune. We alfo fometimes had
invitations from the Spaniards to their
country-houfes. We had a numerous
acquaintance in the city, and in general
received many civilities from the inhabitants. There are a great many people
of fafhion, and very good families from
Old Spain fettled here. A lady lived next
door to us, whofe name was donna Fran-
cifca Giron; and as my name founded

Q 3   fome-

fomething like it, fhe would have it that
we were Parientes. She had a daughter,
a very fine young woman, who both
played and fung remarkably well: fhe
was reckoned the fineft voice in St. Jago.
They faw a great deal of company, and
we were welcome to her houfe whenever we pleafed. We were a long time
in this country, but we paffed it very
agreeably. The prefident alone goes
with four horfes to his coach ; but the
common vehicle here is a calafh, or kind
of vis-à-vis, drawn by one mule only.
Bull-feafts are a common diverfion here,
and they far furpafs any thing of that
kind I ever faw at Lifbon, or any where
elfe. Indeed, it is amazing to fee the activity and dexterity of thofe who attack
the bulls. It is always done here by
thofe only who follow it as a trade, for
it is too dangerous to be practifed as a
diverfion ; as a proof of which, it is
found, that though fome may hold out

longer

longer than others, there are few who conftantly practife it, that die a natural death. The bulls are always the wildeft that can be brought in from the mountains or forefts, and have nothing on their horns to prevent their piercing a man the firft ftroke, as they have at Lifbon. I have feen a man, when the bull came at him with the utmoft fury, fpring directly over the beaft's head, and perform this feat feveral times, and at laft jump on his back, and there fit a confiderable time, the bull the whole time attempting every means to throw him. But though this practitioner was fuccefsful, feveral accidents happened while I was there. The ladies, at thefe feafts, are always dreffed as fine as poffible; and, I imagine, go rather to be admired than to receive any amufement from a fight that one fhould think would give them pain. Another amufement for the ladies here, are the nights of their

Q 4   great

great proceffions, when they go out
veiled ; and as in that drefs they cannot
be known, they amufe themfelves in
talking to people much in the manner that is done at our mafquerades.
One night in Lent, as I was ftanding clofe
to the houfes as the proceffion went by,
and having nothing but a thin waiftcoat
on under my cloak, and happening to
have my arm out, a lady came by, and
gave me a pinch with fo good a will,
that I thought fhe had taken the piece
out ; and, indeed, I carried the marks
for a long time after. I durft not take
the leaft notice of this at the time ; for
had I made any difturbance, I fhould
have been knocked on the head. This
kind lady immediately after mixed with
the crowd, and I never could find
out who had done me that favour. I
have feen fifty or fixty penitents following thefe proceffions ; they wear
a long white garment with a long train

to

to it, and high caps of the fame, which fall down before, and cover all their faces, having only two fmall holes for their eyes; fo that they are never known. Their backs are bare, and they lafh them-felves with a cat-o'-nine-tails till the long train behind is covered all over with blood. Others follow them with great heavy croffes upon their backs; fo that they groan under the weight as they walk barefooted, and often faint away. The ftreets fwarm with friars of all the different orders. The prefident has always a guard at his palace regularly cloathed. The reft of their forces con-fifts of militia, who are numerous.

All European goods are very dear. Englifh cloth of fourteen or fifteen fhil-lings a yard, fells there for ten or eleven dollars; and every other article in pro-portion. We found many Spaniards here that had been taken by commodore Anfon, and had been for fome time prifoners

foners on board the Centurion. They all fpoke in the higheft terms of the kind treatment they had received ; and it is natural to imagine, that it was chiefly owing to that laudable example of humanity our reception here was fo good. They had never had any thing but privateers and buccaneers amongft them before, who handled their prifoners very roughly ; fo that the Spaniards in general, both of Peru and Chili, had the greateft dread of being taken by the Englifh ; but fome of them told us, that they were fo happy on board the Centurion, that they fhould not have been forry if the commodore had taken them with him to England.

After we had been here fome time, Mr. Campbell changed his religion, and of courfe left us. At the end of two years, the prefident fent for us, and informed us a French fhip from Lima, bound to Spain, had put into Valparaifo, and

and that we fhould embark in her.
After taking leave of our good friend
Mr. Gedd, and all our acquaintance at
St. Jago, we fet out for Valparaifo,
mules and a guide being provided for
us. I had forgot to fay before, that
captain Cheap had been allowed by the
prefident fix reals a day, and we had
four for our maintenance the whole
time we were at St. Jago, which money
we took up as we wanted it. Our journey back was much pleafanter than we
found it when we were firft brought
hither, as we had now no mules to drive.
The firft perfon I met, upon our entrance
into Valparaifo, was the poor foldier
whom I mentioned to have been fo kind
to us when we were imprifoned in the
fort. I now made him a little prefent,
which, as it came quite unexpected,
made him very happy. We took lodgings till the fhip was ready to fail, and
diverted ourfelves as we pleafed, having
the

the good fortune, at this time, to have nothing to do with the governor or his fort. The town is but a poor little place; there are, indeed, a good many ſtorehouſes built by the water-ſide for the reception of goods from the ſhipping.

About the 20th of December, 1744, we embarked on board the Lys frigate, belonging to St. Malo. She was a ſhip of four hundred and twenty tons, ſixteen guns, and ſixty men. She had ſeveral paſſengers on board; and amongſt the reſt, don George Juan, a man of very ſuperior abilities (and ſince that time well known in England) who with don Antonio Ulloa had been ſeveral years in Peru, upon a deſign of meaſuring ſome degrees of the meridian near the equator. We were now bound to Conception, in order to join three other French ſhips that were likewiſe bound home. As this was a time of the year when the

ſoutherly

foutherly winds prevail upon this coaft, we ftood off a long way to the weftward, making the ifland of Juan Fernandez. We did not get into the bay of Conception till the 6th of January 1745, where we anchored at Talcaguana, and there found the Louis Erafme, the Marquis d'Antin, and the Delivrance, the three French fhips that we were to accompany. It is but fixty leagues from Valparaifo to Conception, though we had been fo long making this paffage; but there is no beating up, near the fhore, againft the foutherly wind, which is the trade, at this feafon, as you are fure to have a lee-current; fo that the quickeft way of making a paffage is to ftand off a hundred and twenty or thirty leagues from the land.

The bay of Conception is a large, fine bay; but there are feveral fhoals in it, and only two good anchoring-places, though a fhip may anchor within a quarter of a

league

league of the town ; but this only in the
very fine months, as you lay much expofed.
The beft anchoring-place is Talcaguana,
the fouthernmoft neck of the bay, in five
or fix fathom water, good holding
ground, and where you are fheltered
from the northerly winds. The town
has no other defence but a low battery,
which only commands the anchoring-
place before it. The country is extremely
pleafant, and affords the greateft plenty
of provifions of all kinds. In fome
excurfions we made daily from Talcaguana, we faw great numbers of very
large fnakes ; but we were told they
were quite harmlefs. I have read fome
former accounts of Chili, by the jefuits,
wherein they tell you that no venomous
creature is to be found in it, and that they
even made the experiment of bringing
bugs here, which died immediately; but I
never was in any place that fwarmed
with them fo much as St. Jago ; and they
have

have a large spider there, whofe bite is
fo venomous, that I have feen from it
fome of the moft fhocking fights I ever
faw in my life; and it certainly proves
mortal, if proper remedies are not applied
in time. I was once bit by one on the
cheek, whilft afleep, and prefently after,
all that part of my face turned as black
as ink. I was cured by the application
of a bluifh kind of ftone (the fame, perhaps, they call the ferpent-ftone in the
Eaft-Indies, and which is a compofition).
The ftone ftuck, for fome time, of itfelf
on my face, and dropping off, was put
into milk till it had digefted the poifon
it had extracted and then applied again
till the pain abated, and I was foon afterwards well, Whilft the fhips remained
at Conception, the people were employed
in killing of cattle and falting them for
the voyage ; and every fhip took on board
as many bullocks and fheep as their
decks could well hold ; and having com-
pleated

pleated their bufinefs here, they failed
the 27th of January; but about eight
days after our fhip fprung a very dangerous leak forward; but fo low, that
there was no poffibility of ftopping it
without returning into port, and lighten-
ing her till they could come at it. Accordingly we feparated from the other
fhips, and made the beft of our way for
Valparaifo, keeping all hands at the
pump night and day, paffengers and all.
However, as it happened, this proved a
lucky circumftance for the Lys, as the
three other fhips were taken; and which
certainly would have been her fate likewife, had fhe kept company with the reft.
As foon as we got into port, they lighten-
ed the fhip forwards, and brought her
by the ftern till they came at the leak,
which was foon ftopped. They made all
the difpatch poffible in compleating the
water again. Whilft at Valparaifo, we
had one of the moft violent fhocks of an

I   earth-

quake that we had ever felt yet. On the
firft of March we put to fea again, the
feafon being already far advanced for
paffing Cape Horn. The next day we
went to an allowance of a quart of
water a day for each man, which continued the whole paffage. We were
obliged to ftand a long way to the weftward; and went to the northward of
Juan Fernandes above a degree, before
we had a wind that we could make any
fouthing with. On the 25th, in the latitude of 46 degrees, we met with a violent hard gale at weft, which obliged us
to lie to under a reefed mainfail for
fome days; and before we got round the
Cape, we had many very hard gales, with
a prodigious fea and conftant thick fnow;
and after being fo long in fo delightful
a climate as Chili, the cold was almoft
infupportable. After doubling the
Cape, we got but flowly to the north-

ward ; and, indeed, at the beft of times, the fhip never went above fix knots ; for fhe was a heavy-going thing. On the 27th of May we croffed the line ; when finding that our water was grown extremely fhort, and that it would be almoft impoffible to reach Europe without a fupply, it was refolved to bear away for Martinico. On the 29th of June, in the morning, we made the ifland of Tobago, and then fhaped a courfe for Martinico ; and on the firft of July, by our reckonings, expected to fee it, but were difappointed. This was imputed to the currents, which, whether they had fet the fhip to the eaftward or weftward, nobody could tell ; but upon looking over the charts, it was imagined, if the current had driven her to the weftward, it muft have been among the Granadillos, which was thought impoffible without feeing any of them, as they are

fo

fo near together, and a moſt dangerous
place for rocks. It was then concluded
we were to the eaſtward, and accordingly
we ſteered S. W. by W. but having run
this courſe for above thirty leagues, and
no land appearing, it was reſolved to
ſtand to the northward till we ſhould
gain the latitude of Porto Rico, and on
the 4th in the evening we made that
iſland ; ſo that it was now certain the
ſhip had been huſtled through the Granadillos in the night, which was, without doubt, as extraordinary a paſſage as
ever ſhip made. It was now reſolved to
go between the iſlands of Porto Rico
and St. Domingo for Cape Francois,
therefore we lay to that night. In the
morning, we made ſail along ſhore ; and
about ten o'clock, as I was walking the
quarter-deck, captain Cheap came out of
the cabin, and told me he had juſt ſeen
a beef-barrel go by the ſhip ; that he

R 2 was

was fure it had but lately been thrown overboard, and that he would venture any wager we faw an Englifh cruizer before long. In about half an hour after, we faw two fail to leeward, from off the quarter-deck; for they kept no look out from the maft head, and we prefently obferved they were in chace of us. The French and Spaniards on board, now began to grow a good deal alarmed, when it fell ftark calm; but not before the fhips had neared us fo much, that we plainly difcerned them to be Englifh men of war; the one a two-decker, the other a twenty-gun fhip. The French had now thoughts, when a breeze fhould fpring up, of running the fhip on fhore upon Porto Rico; but when they came to confider what a fet of banditti inhabited that ifland, and that in all probability they would have their throats cut for the fake of plunder-

ing

ing the wreck, they were refolved to take
their chance, and ftand to the northward
between the two iflands.   In the evening, a frefh breeze fprung up, and we
fhaped a courfe accordingly.   The two
fhips had it prefently afterwards, and
neared us amazingly faft.   Now every
body on board gave themfelves up ; the
officers were bufy in their cabins, filling
their pockets with what was moft valuable ; the men put on their beft cloaths,
and many of them came to me with
little lumps of gold, defiring I would
take them, as they faid they had much
rather I fhould benefit by them, whom
they were acquainted with, than thofe
that chaced them.   I told them
there was time enough, though I
thought they were as furely taken as if
the Englifh had been already on board.
A fine moonlight night came on, and we
expected every moment to fee the fhips

along-fide of us ; but we faw nothing
of them in the night, and to our great
aftonifhment, in the morning no fhips
were to be feen even from the maft-head.
Thus did thefe two cruizers lofe one of
the richeft prizes, by not chacing an
hour or two longer. There were near
two millions of dollars on board, befides
a valuable cargo. On the eighth, at fix
in the morning, we were off Cape La
Grange ; and, what is very remarkable,
the French at Cape Francois told us afterwards that was the only day they ever
remembered fince the war, that the
Cape had been without one or two Englifh privateers cruifing off it ; and but
the evening before, two of them had
taken two outward-bound St. Domingo
men, and had gone with them for Ja-
maica ; fo that this fhip might be juftly
efteemed a moft lucky one. In the afternoon we came to an anchor in Cape
Francois harbour,

In

In this long run we had not buried
a single man; nor do I remember that
there was one sick the whole passage;
but at this place many were taken ill,
and three or four died; for there is no
part of the West-Indies more unhealthy
than this; yet the country is beautiful,
and extremely well cultivated. After
being here some time, the governor ordered us to wait upon him,
which we did; when he took no
more notice of us than if we had been
his slaves, never asking us even to sit
down.

Towards the end of August a French
squadron of five men of war came in,
commanded by monsieur L'Etanducre,
who were to convoy the trade to France.
Neither he nor his officers ever took
any kind of notice of captain Cheap,
though we met them every day ashore.
One evening, as we were going aboard

R 4 with

with the captain of our ſhip, a midſhip-
man belonging to monſieur L'Etanducre,
jumped into our boat, and ordered the
people to carry him on board the ſhip he
belonged to, leaving us to wait upon the
beach for two hours before the boat returned. On the ſixth of September, we
put to ſea, in company with the five men
of war, and about fifty ſail of merchant-
men. On the eighth we made the
Cayco Grande; and the next day a Ja-
maica privateer, a large fine ſloop, hove
in ſight, keeping a little to windward of
the convoy, reſolving to pick up one or
two of them in the night, if poſſible.
This obliged monſieur L'Etanducre to
ſend a frigate to ſpeak to all the convoy,
and order them to keep cloſe to him in
the night; which they did, and in ſuch
a manner, that ſometimes ſeven or eight
of them were on board one another together; by which they received much
damage;

damage; and to repair which, the whole
squadron was obliged to lay to sometimes for a whole day. The privateer
kept her station, jogging on with the
fleet. At last, the commodore ordered
two of his best-going ships to chace her.
She appeared to take no notice of them
till they were pretty near her, and then
would make sail and be out of sight
presently. The chacing ships no sooner
returned, than the privateer was in company again. As by this every night
some accident happened to some of the
convoy by keeping so close together, a
fine ship of thirty guns, belonging to
Marseilles, hauled out a little to windward of the rest of the fleet; which
L'Etanducre perceiving in the morning,
ordered the frigate to bring the captain
of her on board of him; and then
making a signal for all the convoy to
close to him, he fired a gun, and hoisted
a red

a red flag at the enfign ftaff; and immediately after the captain of the merchant-
man was run up to the main-yard-arm,
and from thence ducked three times.
He was then fent on board his fhip again,
with orders to keep his colours flying
the whole day, in order to diftinguifh
him from the reft. We were then told,
that the perfon who was treated in this
cruel manner, was a young man of an
exceeding good family in the fouth of
France, and likewife a man of great
fpirit; and that he would not fail to
call monfieur L'Etanducre to an account
when an opportunity fhould offer; and
the affair made much noife in France
afterwards. One day, the fhip we were
in happened to be out of her ftation, by
failing fo heavily, when the commodore
made the fignal to fpeak to our captain,
who feemed frightened out of his wits.
When we came near him, he began with
the

the groffeft abufe, threatening our captain, that if ever he was out of his ftation again, he would ferve him as he had done the other. This rigid difcipline, however, preferved the convoy; for though the privateer kept company a long time, fhe was not fo fortunate as to meet with the reward of her perfeverance.

On the 27th of October, in the evening, we made Cape Ortegal; and on the 31ft, came to an anchor in Breft road. The Lys having fo valuable a cargo on board, was towed into the harbour the next morning, and lafhed alongfide one of their men of war. The money was foon landed; and the officers and men, who had been fo many years abfent from their native country, were glad to get on fhore. Nobody remained on board but a man or two to look after the fhip, and we three Englifh prifoners, who had

no

no leave to go afhore. The weather was extremely cold, and felt particularly fo to us, who had been fo long ufed to hot climates; and what made it ftill worfe, we were very thinly clad. We had nei- ther fire nor candle; for they were al- lowed on board of no fhip in the har- bour, for fear of accidents, being clofe to their magazines in the dock-yard. Some of the officers belonging to the fhip were fo kind to fend us off victuals every day, or we might have ftarved; for mon- fieur L'Intendant never fent us even a meffage; and though there was a very large fquadron of men of war fitting out at that time, not one officer belonging to them ever came near captain Cheap. From five in the evening we were ob- liged to fit in the dark; and if we chofe to have any fupper, it was neceffary to place it very near us before that time, or we never could have found it. We

6   had

had paffed feven or eight days in this melancholy manner, when one morning a kind of row-galley came along-fide with a number of Englifh prifoners belonging to two large privateers the French had taken. We were ordered into the fame boat with them, and were carried four leagues up the river to Landernaw. At this town we were upon our parole; fo took the beft lodgings we could get, and lived very well for three months, when an order came from the court of Spain to allow us to return home by the firft fhip that offered. Upon this, hearing there was a Dutch fhip at Morlaix ready to fail, we took horfes and travelled to that town, where we were obliged to remain fix weeks, before we had an opportunity of getting away. At laft we agreed with the mafter of a Dutch dogger to land us at Dover, and paid him before-hand. When

we

we had got down the river into the
road, a French privateer that was almoſt
ready to ſail upon a cruize, hailed the
Dutchman, and told him to come to an
anchor; and that if he offered to ſail before him, he would ſink him. This he
was forced to comply with, and lay
three days in the road, curſing the
Frenchman, who at the end of that time
put to ſea, and then we were at liberty
to do the ſame. We had a long uncomfortable paſſage. About the ninth
day, before ſun-ſet, we ſaw Dover, and
reminded the Dutchman of his agree-
ment to land us there. He ſaid he
would; but inſtead of that, in the morning we were off the coaſt of France.
We complained loudly of this piece of
villany, and inſiſted upon his returning
to land us, when an Engliſh man of war
appeared to windward, and preſently
bore down to us. She ſent her boat on
board

board with an officer, who informed us
the fhip he came from was the Squirrel,
commanded by captain Mafterfon. We
went on board of her, and captain Mafterfon immediately fent one of the cut-
ters he had with him, to land us at
Dover, where we arrived that afternoon,
and directly fet out for Canterbury upon
poft-horfes; but captain Cheap was fo
tired by the time he got there, that he
could proceed no further that night.
The next morning he ftill found himfelf fo much fatigued, that he could ride
no longer; therefore it was agreed that
he and Mr. Hamilton fhould take a poft-
chaife, and that I fhould ride; but here
an unlucky difficulty was ftarted; for
upon fharing the little money we had, it
was found to be not fufficient to pay the
charges to London; and my proportion
fell fo fhort, that it was, by calculation,
barely enough to pay for horfes, with-

out

out a farthing for eating a bit upon the road, or even for the very turnpikes. Thofe I was obliged to defraud, by riding as hard as I could through them all, not paying the leaft regard to the men, who called out to ftop me. The want of refrefhment I bore as well as I could. When I got to the Borough, I took a coach and drove to Marlborough-ftreet, where my friends had lived when I left England; but when I came there, I found the houfe fhut up. Having been abfent fo many years, and in all that time never having heard a word from home, I knew not who was dead, or who was living, or where to go next; or even how to pay the coachman. I recollected a linen-draper's fhop, not far from thence, which our family had ufed. I therefore drove there next, and making myfelf known, they paid the coachman. I then enquired after our family, and

was

was told my fifter had married lord Car-
lifle, and was at that time in Soho-
fquare. I immediately walked to the
houfe, and knocked at the door ; but
the porter not liking my figure, which
was half French, half Spanifh, with the
addition of a large pair of boots covered
with dirt, he was going to fhut the door
in my face; but I prevailed with him
to let me come in.

I need not acquaint my readers with
what furprife and joy my fifter received
me. She immediately furnifhed me with
money fufficient to appear like the reft of
my countrymen; till that time I could
not be properly faid to have finifhed all
the extraordinary fcenes which a feries
of unfortunate adventures had kept me
in for the fpace of five years and upwards.

F   I   N   I   S,

Lightning Source UK Ltd.
Milton Keynes UK
UKOW04f1144160913

217281UK00001B/12/P